D0561857

The Black Quarterback Syndrome
How to Succeed as a First or Pioneer in an Organization

Norman M. Davis

Organizational & Diversity
Consulting & Publishing, LLC
New Haven, CT

Library of Congress Cataloging-in-Publication Data is available through the Library of Congress

© Norman M. Davis
ISBN#978-0-9816865-5-4

Published 2009 by Organizational & Diversity Consulting & Publishing LLC

Cover photographer – Ron Waite. Chairman of the Communications Department, Albertus Magnus College

Printed by You 2 Books Publishing Company, LLC
179 Allyn Street, suite 507
Hartford, CT 06103
www.you2books.com
(860) 724-2233 (888) GLORY-90

Biographical Information

Norman M. Davis, Ph.D., is a management professor, organizational trainer and consultant, and a public speaker. He specializes in human resources, teambuilding, diversity, and new-manager assimilation. His previous writing has been mainly newspaper editorials on a variety of topics. With more than 20 years of corporate and management experience, naturally many of his observations and analyses come from his years of consulting with management and employees to resolve a variety of employee relations and organizational problems. Dr. Davis was elected to Who's Who Among Executives and Professionals in 2009.

Dedication

This management book is written for the many people who are or will be the first individuals like themselves who have been hired into an organization or into a particular position in an organization. They are pioneers who may need trail maps to guide them toward survival and ultimate success. Although there are many survivors of the climb up the organizational ladder, many do not make it. This book is written to be a quick but comprehensible read — a "how to" and reference book, to help you in your climb up the ladder or in your desire to help others climb that ladder.

Interviews with individuals and acquaintances who have reached their goals have been used. You'll find snippets of their impressive histories at the end of chapter 5. I thank them all for their enrichment of these pages.

Your World

Your world is as big as you make it.

I know, for I used to abide

In the narrowest nest in the corner,

My wings pressing close to my side.

But I sighted the distant horizon

Where the skyline encircled the sea

And I throbbed with a burning desire

To travel this immensity.

I battered the cordons around me

And cradled my wings on the breeze

Then to the uttermost reaches

With rapture, with power, with ease!

— Georgia Douglas Johnson 1880 – 1966

Harlem Renaissance poet

CONTENTS

**The Black Quarterback Syndrome:
How to Succeed as a First or Pioneer in an Organization**

Part III:
The 12 Steps to Success for Pioneers

About the Cover

The photo on the cover of this book is a staged and literal example of the black quarterback syndrome (BQS), a metaphor that will be further explained and explored throughout the book's pages. I'm thrilled that, in my life time, the American public has been able to challenge such a metaphor so wholeheartedly that it has elected Barack Obama, the first black president of the United States of America.

Moreover, you may have noticed that the business-dressed woman is neither black nor a quarterback and that too is an important part of the BQS metaphor; anyone in an organization might experience the black quarterback syndrome. They just need to be one of the"firsts" in their position or in the organization.

The cover models are from Albertus Magnus College and are from left to right, Andrew Foster, Director of Financial Aid; Jennifer Pacelli, Director of Athletics; and Lemuel Soto, student majoring in Computer Information Systems.

"Although this book speaks to the leveling of organizational playing fields rather than the football playing fields, I could have used it for personal companionship on many a lonely night and for its survival strategies as a first and pioneer."

Marlin Briscoe, First black National Football League
starting quarterback

Part I: The Black Quarterback Syndrome

Introduction

How First NFL Starting Black Quarterback Marlin Briscoe Named a Syndrome

Join me for a moment on a brief organizational excursion. Imagine a fellow named Bill. We've all known or met a Bill at one time or another. He's the guy you've worked with who was really talented, but for some reason never recognized his own abilities. It would be more accurate to say that he had no clue about how good he was. Although he thought he was okay, there was something deep inside that kept him looking back over his shoulder, comparing himself unfavorably to the other co-workers who were performing in the very same position as himself. This was not the right outlook for success in the youth-dominated, competitive corporate environment into which Bill had been promoted.

Unfortunately, Bill was swimming in doubt, primarily, because he did not have a bachelor's degree from college. For years, only individuals with bachelor's degrees or higher were given the opportunity of holding this entry-level professional position. Bill was the first person promoted from the inside or hired from the outside for this position, who did not have a college degree. He had many years of related work experience but quite frankly, he and many others throughout the company had been stalled with an out-of-date attitude that it took a college degree to perform successfully in the position. There were many lower level employees who quietly questioned among themselves whether and why a college degree was necessary for the position. In the more recent years of exploding technology there seemed to be a drastically reduced need for higher education. In reality, knowledge of the company, customer service skills, and personal poise were the most important requisites.

The core responsibility of Bill's position was to provide customer service to internal employee clients or outside customers about the company's products and services. Interestingly, as well as sadly, he always felt personally at fault for not being clear enough on these issues. Bill stewed over any client's confusion and wondered if his lack of a college degree was at the root of his apparent inability to eliminate all client questions. When Bill received corrective or negative performance feedback, he wondered if the manager was being totally honest and if something was being left out of the performance evaluation. He thought that perhaps the manager preferred to have someone with a college degree in the position that he held. The manager never said so, but he felt that the company had demonstrated their preference by previously always hiring college graduates for the position.

Bill began to press and become overly nervous with internal and external customers. He constantly wondered to himself if management or others doubted him as he doubted himself, and he believed deeply that if they did it was certainly because he did not have a college degree. He began to play the day's comments and events over in his mind each evening and questioned inwardly which co-workers wanted to see him succeed. He began to envision a scenario in which another co-worker with a degree would be brought in and he would be demoted to his former position in a face-saving move for him as well as management. Bill continued to engage in doubt, loss of confidence, and loss of poise. Often he would see others — peers, clients, and management — talking with each other, and wonder if they were meeting about him and the fact that he did not have a college degree.

A number of his co-workers and managers sensed from Bill's comments and behaviors that the lack of a college degree must be an issue for Bill in some way. They understood that no one had ever held this position without a college degree and with the degree it seemed that nearly everyone had succeeded. Of course, a few people with college degrees failed, but they knew that could happen with any person and in any position. Interestingly, a few co-workers and managers felt strongly that a college degree was clearly not necessary. They wanted Bill to succeed, and even felt some sympathy for his situation, but they did not dare to ever mention this to him for fear that it might cause him to be upset or more concerned about his lack of a degree. As a result they pretended not to notice Bill's increasing self-doubt and growing discomfort. Bill suffered from what I have come to call the black quarterback syndrome (BQS). I contend that these circumstances are more common than most of us realize and that they are a problem for employees and management in many organizations. Too often such circumstances go unspoken and, furthermore, unresolved. In many ways it does not matter who is at fault because what we have is an employee struggling with performance issues, a barrier to full organizational participation, and therefore, ultimately a waste of individual talent, company recruiting, selection, and training efforts.

***

I am a keen observer of organizations, their employees, and their management. Furthermore, I was fortunate to have been an executive with a large insurance company for many years, and, for the past 12 years, I have been a management professor at Albertus Magnus College in New Haven, Connecticut. Additionally, during the last 15 years as an organizational consultant, I've kept up with the evolution of the workplace.

I am particularly motivated to write about work topics that are seldom if ever discussed among employees and managers in organizations or even discussed in books. My personal experiences have compelled me to share a variety of observations. Many of those observations began when I was a manager of Personnel and Management Consulting for a large and successful diversified financial corporation that employed more than 45,000 people in the early 1980s. I managed a staff of consultants who met with management and employees and counseled them on resolving their problems, issues, and concerns. In doing so, I was either directly or indirectly through my staff, responsible for resolving more than 10,000 cases over a 10-year period. I was privileged to work with a variety of employees, some who were "superstars," and others who were performance liabilities. I worked with employees and managers whose tenure was longer than I had lived. I worked with people of all races and various ethnic groups, and graduates from the most prestigious colleges as well as high-school dropouts. I observed gifted managers, average managers, and those who struggled to master the skill of getting work done by using other people, the meaning of managing. I observed confident and competent workers as well as dour imposters and a few who asked to be relieved of the "hassles" and "challenges" of managing. I saw careers rise like rockets and other careers sputter like wet firecrackers. I have even seen some careers start on a good track and reverse to a bad track, and then revert back to their original good postures.

Furthermore, I also observed the passage of the Civil Rights Act of 1964, which introduced Affirmative Action, just before I graduated from college. I recall the heightened expectations and the subsequent implementation of Affirmative Action as I began my own professional career in 1967. I observed Affirmative Action from the inside as a potential beneficiary (I am black and male) and from a good vantage point as a human resources professional in the 1980s. In that role, I was required to understand Affirmative Action, and in some cases help implement it. I saw many organizations and employees struggle, some making strong good faith efforts and others making little effort to understand and accomplish the goals of Affirmative Action whether from the Government's perspective or from their organization's perspective. For years I found that graduating college students, whether minority or white, had remarkably varied knowledge of Affirmative Action. In each succeeding decade after the passage of Affirmative Action legislation, much of the promise and excitement of the late 60s began to convert to legal, political, and philosophical discussions.

From my vantage point, few colleges provided education about Affirmative Action, and if they did, it was for human resource majors. Most of the information was obtained from anecdotal sources like professors, friends, television, and newspapers covering discrimination lawsuits and the like, but not textbooks. Even now, more than 40 years later, I find that Affirmative Action is covered in textbooks in a much too dry, matter-of-fact, and legal manner. Seldom is Affirmative Action described as the federal government's administrative and ethical process to correct the enormous number and egregious inequities that existed in the workplace prior to 1964. Factually speaking, women and minorities did not have nearly as many opportunities as they do today. Interestingly, I predict that the opportunities of today in business and politics will be viewed 20 years from now, as indeed, paltry. My professional experiences as a manager, management professor, and consultant, combined with personal experiences, have given me a unique platform. In this book I seek to share this rare knowledge with the employees, managers, and students who want to add to their organization and management knowledge. The method of sharing is to introduce the reader to an easily comprehended metaphor that will be understood and remembered for years, unlike many of the esoteric complicated books on management and management theory that abound.

By now you may be asking, "What is the black quarter-back syndrome?" How could "anyone" relate to a syndrome that suggests that you must be black or a quarterback when 99.99999 % of people in America do not meet these two factors? Let me answer these questions with a little background that goes back to the end of the 1960s.

It was late fall of 1968 and I was one year out of the University of Nebraska, Omaha. I had just moved to New Haven, Connecticut, from Rockford, Illinois, my hometown, searching for more career opportunities. Rockford was a manufacturing city of approximately 136,000 people. This conservative midwestern city was known for making machine tools and was the home of Ingersoll Milling Company, Woodward Governor, Barber Coleman Company, and Sundstrand Aviation. All of these companies were great places for college graduates interested in the engineering and technical fields, but not for me, a general education major with few clues about careers or career opportunities. I was the first in my family to graduate from college and the general thinking had been to find a job and work in the same company until retirement, 35 or 40 years later. However, just one year later, after working in one of the most interesting and progressive jobs I would ever have, the Singer Zone Mental Health Hospital, I relocated to New Haven.

That fall, a Monday evening sports television story in New Haven was about a rookie black National Football League (NFL) quarterback, Marlin Briscoe, and how he had gone into a game with only 10 minutes left to play and led the Denver Broncos from a 20 to 7 deficit to nearly win the game. Briscoe completed his first three passes, scrambled for a touchdown, and then, on a subsequent possession, moved the team down the field to score a field goal, although they finally lost 20 to 17. The game culminated with Denver fans in a wild frenzy. The Broncos had lost their first two games and up until Briscoe's heroics, the offense had looked anemic. But now fans and players had hope. Hope from a scrambling black quarterback who in college was dubbed "The Magician." He almost pulled a rabbit out of his hat in those thrilling 10 minutes. That Briscoe was black just seemed to add a little more spice to the story as reported on television that night. Denver was even anticipating another 25,000 fans for next week's game and Briscoe's first start, which would be a history-making event. This would be the first start for a black quarterback in the NFL ever.

Most people at that time thought Marlin Briscoe was the first black quarterback to play in the NFL. However, in 1953, the Chicago Bears' regular quarterback, George Blanda, was hurt and Willie Thrower, a quarterback from Michigan State University, got into the game in the fourth quarter but never started or played quarterback again according to a 2002 Associated Press story available online at ESPN Classic. Marlin Briscoe became the first starting black quarterback and went on to start seven games during that history-making season. Some might wonder today what the big deal was for a black guy to be playing quarterback. With the number of black athletes in pro sports today and, indeed, the number of black quarterbacks as well in the NFL, they might say "Who cares?" Well, in 1968, a lot of people cared for a lot of different reasons. As a college professor today, I know that white and even minority college students find it hard to understand and appreciate what is was like for Briscoe.

The primary reason people cared was that there was an unspoken issue, if not belief, for many that blacks could not lead whites on the football field. Many believed that white players would not follow the directions of a black quarterback. Furthermore, there were doubters who believed that the black quarterback could not be smart enough to handle the leadership role, and since black players were not given the chance to prove otherwise, there was a lack of evidence to the contrary. I should add now, but will comment later in greater detail, that I discovered, over the next 25 years, that the same unspoken thoughts existed in the business world about blacks, other minorities, women or other first-of-a kind pioneers when it came to giving them managerial or other significant positions of responsibility. When Marlin Briscoe joined the Denver football training camp in 1968 it was as the last and lowest-rated of eight quarterbacks. If you read his book, *The First Black Quarterback*, and I hope you will, it will be apparent that from his midget football days until college, Briscoe encountered one event after another in which seemingly well-meaning whites in Omaha, Nebraska, tried to steer him away from playing quarterback. I say "well-meaning" because they were, but there seemed to be an ignorance born of not having seen a black athlete play quarterback. These individuals encouraged Briscoe to play football; however, he would be asked to leave the quarterback practice line and move to the running back line where they thought he would be more suited to play. Fortunately, he was determined to play quarterback and was able to prove himself each time he was given a fair chance. It is important that we give individuals a fair chance to pursue what they strongly believe they can do. This is a significant management principal and it is also related to helping others achieve their aspirations. I am reminded of how persons without disabilities in the workplace often underestimate what a person with a disability and strong desire can achieve.

At some point in the early 1970s, I saw an article in the New Haven Register that featured blind snow skiers who were Vietnam War veterans at the West Haven Veterans Medical Center. I was so surprised, (actually I was amazed) that I became a volunteer with their program and invited them to my apartment for beverages. These men weren't surprised by themselves at all. They simply had a very strong desire to learn to ski. Sighted individuals, managers, and team members should recognize that when people have a strong interest in doing something, with support, they often can learn to do it.

In his book, Briscoe explained that it was only after some injuries to other quarterbacks ahead of him, shrewd contract negotiating, mediocre play by those in front of him, and pressure from Denver fans, that he got his chance to play leader or NFL quarterback.

Every Sunday and Monday for the remainder of the season, I would seek news on whether Briscoe played quarterback and how he did. He and I had played on the basketball team together for a while at Nebraska Omaha. We were friends and I even sublet my apartment to him one summer when I returned home to Rockford. It was natural that I would have a strong interest in his play and success. I really wanted him to do well. But I noticed something just as strong within me when James Harris (quarterback for the Washington Redskins), Randall Cunningham (quarterback for the Philidelphia Eagles), and others were drafted and fighting for their positions and opportunities to play quarterback.

I noticed that my feelings were just as strong and supportive of these new black quarterbacks as they were for my friend and college mate, Marlin Briscoe. I found myself pleading emotionally for these guys to make every third down play, complete every pass, execute every play flawlessly, look and lead confidently. I emotionally died when they fumbled or were intercepted. I felt a personal need for them to succeed. I found myself wanting them to succeed even against my favorite teams. I would listen closely to the way the announcers described their performance and sometimes would take affront if the announcer implied that the black quarterback was having trouble reading the defense or criticized their execution of a play. I began to ask myself why I was taking the black quarterback performance so personally and feeling that if they failed it would be a failure for our race, thus suggesting that we couldn't be leaders or managers of white players.

For so many, the football field (in an unspoken manner), turned into a proving ground to demonstrate that black quarterbacks were smart enough; that white and other black players could believe in their abilities to lead, manage, and play the quarterback position. During the first few years of blacks playing quarterback, not once did I hear anyone, black or white, express these sentiments. It was not discussable. Today we can have these discussions and I offer this as an example of racial progress in the United States. Of course, there are many other examples. Personally, I was certain that a black athlete could handle quarterback responsibilities in high school, college, or the NFL if given the opportunity. I knew about blacks having to prove that they could be soldiers in World Wars I and II; Tuskegee Airmen having to prove they could fly airplanes and be World War II pilots; blacks needing to prove they could be school teachers in predominantly white school systems in northern cities during the 40s, 50s and 60s; blacks proving that they could be major league baseball players; proving that they could be actors; and, as in the case of my brother, who proved that he could be the first black gas station attendant in Rockford, Illinois, in 1958, doing that too. When my brother became the gas station attendant while waiting to begin his freshman year in college, it was seen as fairly significant by the black community. Fortunately, my brother saw it as a nothing special and recently retired as an instrument designer in the Department of Astronomy and the Steward Observatory at the University of Arizona. Recalling stories like this one can enable one to see how societal and perhaps even community expectations can sometimes be quite limiting.

I comprehended the skepticism directed toward aspiring black quarterbacks. However, during high school and college, I simply had been around too many smart, athletic, and capable black athletes to have the slightest doubt that they were capable of playing quarterback. I understood that many whites, and even some blacks, needed to see black quarterbacks succeed on the field or on their televisions before they could accept that it could be allowed, tolerated, and accomplished.

I found myself having discussions with friends and co-workers about football in ways previously not discussed. People were saying things about how great it was to watch a black quarterback play and they talked about whether black quarterbacks scrambled too much or whether they had the mentality to be able to stay in the pocket and throw, and whether they could read the complicated defenses or execute the complicated offensive systems of some coaches. Now some of this is natural football talk that would occur with any novice quarterback, but it took on a special sensitivity because there had been so few black quarterbacks. There were many people, whites and blacks, who verbally supported the new black quarterbacks. Many football fans were selecting teams to be their favorite because they had a black quarterback or would simply favor the team with the black quarterback. The reasons varied for why people were supportive of these new black quarterbacks: it was good for the game, it was new and fresh, they played the position differently, you never knew what might happen next, and any number of other reasons, including "I just want the black quarterback to win" or "I want him to lose." Often blacks and whites were similarly supportive or doubtful of the black quarterback's knowledge, skills, or abilities. And often, the reasoning was unspoken and therefore undiscussable.

As I assessed my own racially biased yet supportive desires for the black quarterback to succeed, I discerned that my own constant need to prove myself professionally in predominantly white organizations was by 1985 a huge factor. I desperately wanted the black quarterback to succeed so that the corporate employees and managers that I worked with would have confidence and trust in the players, employees, leaders, or black quarterbacks in America's organizations. When I say black quarterbacks in the context of corporate America, I mean blacks who were new to holding certain leadership, supervisory, or managerial positions or simply were new to holding certain positions in an organization or an industry. Being made the first black marketing manager in the company or the first black pharmaceutical representative in the region could result in facing the black quarterback syndrome. Being the first black lawyer in the corporation or the first director of human resources could put you into the black quarterback syndrome. Or being the first black receptionist or the first black vice president in investment banking could thrust you into the black quarterback syndrome. Actually, all people who are different, yet pioneers, could find themselves faced with the black quarterback syndrome (BQS).

"Good breeding consists in concealing how much we think of ourselves and how little we think of the other person." **Mark Twain**

Chapter 1

What Is the Black Quarterback Syndrome?

All of the emotion and pressure bottled up in fans is nothing compared to the emotion and pressure that the black NFL quarterback himself experiences. First, and most important, is the pressure to execute and perform at the highest level and to do it consistently. Doing this with 250- to 350-pound linemen wishing to crush your soul on every play would be enormous pressure for any sane person. The black quarterback syndrome (BQS) is the additional pressure, real or imagined, above the regular football performance pressures that a black quarterback will feel. It is also the emotional sum of all the life events that remind him that he was different from others who played the position before him.

Dealing With Extreme Pressure in Sports

It is necessary to say at this point that successful athletic performers seldom speak about or dwell on the pressure present in the work they do. To do so would be to begin to invite another opponent into the game — doubt. Proud athletes do not speak of pressure. Additionally, they are certainly not likely to acknowledge the kind of sociological, psychological, and societal pressures associated with race that when spoken aloud is done at risk. This is a risk that most black employees at any level in any organization, including sports, have learned it is better to avoid. What is the risk? It is the risk of not being understood, the risk of being seen as whining, or the risk of being charged with the now famous line from the O. J. Simpson trial, "Playing the race card." That line suggests to me that any time that race is used to explain something or is stated as the reason why something is taking place, the person offering race as the factor is using an illegitimate reason or an unethical rationale. I suppose some think that line is cute, made for television, but the implications are grossly unfair and wrong. Explanations should be evaluated on their merit for that is how we come to learn and understand behavior. When I hear someone declare that the race card is being played, I hear a lack of interest or desire to listen carefully enough to get the truth of the situation. If after careful listening to an employee's explanation, a manager determines that the employee is using race as an excuse for lack of performance, then he or she should say so and address that issue. Accusations of playing the race card are, in my opinion, examples of lazy articulation and incomplete methods that further complicate and distance race relations.

Despite the insights that I have sought to provide, few successful minority workers acknowledge privately or publicly to their management or team members that their racial circumstances bring them extra pressure and ask for patience and support on the job. When the black quarterback adapts this way, by putting a quieting lid on any expression of this pressure, he simply adds another source of internal pressure with which he must cope, which adds profoundly to the pressure-cooker nature of being among the first. Conversely, for the black quarterback to have someone in whom he can trust and discuss his performance in playing the positions becomes very important. Indeed, it is this simmering pressure that will not be discussed that further comprises the black quarterback syndrome. The black quarterback has the extra pressure of being different from white quarterbacks and additionally has the pressure of having to pretend that this does not matter or add any additional pressure.

Interestingly, I have noticed that the most prominent and successful blacks, whether in sports or corporations, seem to be less likely to speak about the racial aspect of their pioneering roles and focus more on the functional aspects of their performance. It seems to be their way of dealing with the BQS and moving forward.

In May 2008, Willie Randolph, the first black manager for the New York Mets baseball team, hinted about the symptoms related to the extra pressure of being a pioneer. In the 2007 baseball season, the Mets lost a large lead in the race to get into the playoffs. They collapsed, thus not making the playoffs. From the beginning of the 2008 season, impatient fans and the New York press were not in the least hesitant to express criticism toward the players and the manager. The fans felt free to boo them when they thought, in their judgment, that it was warranted. In an interview with Ian O'Connor, reporter from the Bergen Record Newspaper, in which the conversation turned toward how the fans viewed the Mets record and Randolph's performance in the new season, the criticism, boos and all, Randolph questioned whether it was "racial"? According to the reporter, when asked if black managers were held to a different standard from white managers, Randolph responded, "I don't know how to put my finger on it, but there's something there. Herman Edwards did pretty well here and he won a couple of playoff [games], and they were pretty hard on Herm. Isiah [Thomas] didn't do a great job but they beat up Isiah pretty good... I don't know if people are used to a certain figurehead. There's something weird about it. I think it's very important…that I handle myself in a way that those [African-American managers] coming behind me will get the opportunities, too…"

The field of performance was baseball, but Willie Randolph experienced the black quarterback syndrome, the wondering, the extra pressure, and how to handle it. The dilemma implicit in the BQS and Randolph's dilemma was how to handle extra pressure, not only internally, but externally. New York sports radio talk shows spoke of the story nearly constantly for three days and took phone calls from the fans. Some fans that called in actually identified themselves by race and some white fans asked how Randolph could introduce the "race card" when it was clear to them that the only issue for them was that the Mets were not winning and therefore Randolph and the Mets were getting what they deserved.

Willie Randolph learned more about what he already knew, and that was that people don't like to hear about challenges or perceptions thought to be related to race.

After several days of additional criticism of Randolph by fans, sports pundits, and sports reporters for having the audacity to introduce race into the dynamics of performance and losing baseball games, Randolph issued an apology. Yes, despite the pain of the original press and fan criticism, which Randolph said "hurt me to my core," he apologized. He found it necessary to cover up any thoughts he had of the extra pressure or BQS because too many fans and press members could not understand that such feelings were legitimate.

Most people determine something to be legitimate if they agree with it, have experienced it, or have personally observed it. So how do you get others to agree with something with which they initially disagree or have never observed? I think the answer is to make them experience it or make them see the potential benefits of understanding the other position. In this case of course I am referring to the importance of understanding the BQS and the potential benefits from learning about and managing its dynamics.

Dealing With Extra Pressure in Business

Certainly by now you have had the thought that everyone who takes a new position will feel some performance pressure. If so, you are correct. However, the individual does not face the pressure of the black quarterback syndrome unless there is, in addition to the performance pressure, the pressure of being so different from others who have had the same position. The first woman director of marketing, the first white writer for Ebony magazine, the first 60-year-old white male program director at MTV, the first Latino vice president of information technology, or the first Asian manager of pharmaceutical sales may experience the black quarterback syndrome. Many non-black employees and managers I have counseled have reluctantly shared the experience of feeling the pressure and symptoms of BQS. While they had no name for their experience, they had come to feel it would be a form of weakness to acknowledge that such a pressure, inhibitor, or barrier existed.

With this new awareness, I was able to see a very personal internal struggle within people. This struggle was different from the struggle of trying to master the responsibilities, tasks, and duties associated with job performance. It seemed to be more a matter of projecting confidence and comfort in the position. If the employees were of a different race, age, or gender, for example, than most people who had ever held such a position, they seemed to carry some extra burden on their shoulders, which I could see in their eyes.

Consider the story of Virginia (name changed), a young, white, female recent college graduate from "one of the better schools," who was among the first women ever hired into the sales force of a prominent insurance company that sold multimillion dollar health insurance contracts to large corporations. Virginia was recruited purposefully to respond to the increased number of women being hired into the professional ranks of both the present client and potential client organizations. Virginia complained of being ignored by the client who favored speaking with the male members of the sales force who had previously serviced the account. In meetings with the client and with her own sales team members she found her male co-worker using the client's preference for a male sales representative in order to highlight his own knowledge and position with the client. Bob, Virginia's male sales team member, gloated over his knowledge of golf. He basked in the attention given him by the client and engaged in behind the scenes discussions with the client about whether women should sell this type of insurance.

Virginia's pressure to succeed came less from learning about and performing her job than from overcoming the pressure she felt from the attitude of her own sales co-workers and the clients. Virginia stopped being the confident college graduate and became reticent and lost confidence. She stewed over her circumstances and grew to resent her co-worker and to fight back grudgingly by trying to sabotage him and make him experience pain also. In effect, Virginia was experiencing the pain and pressure of the black quarterback syndrome and she either selected or drifted into behaviors that destined her to fail at her job, despite being extraordinarily knowledgeable and capable.

Another story concerns Tyler (name changed), a black male from a prestigious Ivy League college. Tyler possessed an MBA degree and was hired by a medium-sized bank after being highly recommended by a headhunter. He had more than 10 years of mortgage-lending experience with a prestigious competitor bank that was even more prestigious than the bank to which Tyler emigrated. Tyler speculated that being a big fish in a small pond might eventually take him farther. Tyler was also not typical in that he had an MBA. His hiring signaled an effort by the bank to seek higher caliber employees and to be more competitive with other banks. Tyler was the first black hired by the bank who had a higher position than teller. These were the circumstances despite the bank's location in a medium-sized banking center with a regional population that was nearly 30% black. Tyler replaced the retiring mortgage loan manager who had only a bachelor's degree. Upon his arrival Tyler was greeted with open envy and wonderment about why the bank had gone outside the organization to fill the position. Tyler was also greeted warmly by some at the middle and senior management levels who often referred to him as the first black officer within the bank and the first symbol of new directions that the bank needed to take in order to compete in the 21st century. Although Tyler was considered to be in middle management, he became extremely visible, appearing in the bank's local and regional advertising and public service announcements, and representing the bank at numerous banking and community-related events. Tyler became the most visible and externally promoted middle manager in the bank.

When the number of mortgages remained stable and customer service ratings slipped, the whispering changed. Rumors about the failure of the "Affirmative Action high-caliber hiring experiment" were traveling the hallways. Employees and some middle managers began to openly question whether a black banker could really understand the bank's culture and history, which was the accumulation of the bank's 80-year residency in the town. "After all, most blacks in the town were sustained through their employment at the local steel foundry and existed on very modest wages from the lower level positions that they were able to acquire," said one vice president to the bank president. Employees who might have been candidates in normal times for Tyler's position began to whisper quite loudly about how Affirmative Action and reverse discrimination were hurting the bank. Needless to say, Tyler could not help but hear them. After his first 6 months at the bank, Tyler suggested that the bank's local and regional advertising, training of loan processors, and processing system were in dire need of upgrading. He was ignored by management and advised to "learn the bank first." The learning period was rapidly ending and becoming a period of constant explanation and defense of why the results were not equal to those of the former manager. As Tyler's confidence continued to fade, he began to see a psychologist, and complained of dizziness and the inability to sleep.

In unraveling his emotions and slipping performance to the psychologist, Tyler confided that race had become an undiscussable issue. From the beginning he felt "highlighted" because of his race. Some of the highlighting was supposed to be positive, "first black, more to come," and some of it was negative, "he wouldn't be here if it weren't for the reverse discrimination of Affirmative Action." Tyler's largest and most painful complaint to the psychologist was that he felt uncertain about how his immediate superior and peers felt about his race, his capabilities, and the rumors pertaining to race and his performance. Furthermore, he felt that he was not supposed to acknowledge this extra pressure that was rooted in race or the black quarterback syndrome that surrounded him.

With help from the psychologist, Tyler sought to express the feelings he withheld, not with the current bank, but with a vice president from the former bank. The warm but open frank discussions led to the former bank officer asking Tyler to return, to which he promptly agreed. These frank discussions resulted in the development of an extraordinarily open and competitive work environment at that bank. Frankness was encouraged at all levels of the organization and on any work-related topic or concern. Tyler emerged as a strong player and leader in this evolving progressive environment. Problems and barriers were constantly being detected and corrected in various areas. Improved customer service, creation of new products, and improvement of old ones, deletion of unprofitable products, reformed benefits, and growth of an even more dynamic company image were some of the employee-driven changes that resulted.

These two examples illustrate how race and gender created the extra pressure on top of everyday performance pressure and from these examples, it can easily be seen how age, ethnicity, handicap, or even sexual preference might lead to the black quarterback syndrome. Indeed, in any circumstance where the employee, new leader, manager, or quarterback is among the "first," there may be a foothold and pathway to the black quarterback syndrome. In effect, psychologists might refer to this as internalized oppression because of being different and first.

After years of noticing the many pressures and similarities that minorities faced in trying to succeed in organizations, I coined the phrase black quarterback syndrome as a metaphor — easily recognized and learned — for the particular situation in which the "firsts" or "pioneers" find themselves in an organization.

However, the point needs to be made that the persons who are the second, third, fourth, fifth, and so on will also find themselves toiling under black quarterback syndrome. I consider those individuals to be near firsts. Moreover, sometimes being "the only one" can lead to feelings of being in the black quarterback syndrome. James Harris, the second NFL starting black quarterback faced many of the challenges that Marlin Briscoe faced years earlier.

In baseball, Larry Doby became the second black major league player and had to face many of the same indignities and pressures that Jackie Robinson faced. Often those who follow the initial "first" actually don't receive as much support as the original first. Sometimes those near firsts are overlooked, as Larry Doby often was. Doby was signed by the Cleveland Indians baseball team just 11 weeks after Jackie Robinson was signed, but his pioneering role in baseball is not known by many. In organizations, it can be the same way. For example, the second female governor of a state might face as many challenges because she is a woman and experience just as much doubt, skepticism, or sexism from the population as the first one did. Sometimes the public response is that since one female governor has been elected, it proves the glass ceiling has been broken and we don't need to support any other women. I find it humorous, naïve, and sometimes bordering on the ridiculous when the news pundits intimate that because Hillary Clinton or Barack Obama did so well with their primary campaigns in 2008, it proves that the people of the United States will now accept either a woman or a black person as their president. Obama's election does not prove that the United States would necessarily accept a black president. Rather, it proves that an extremely well-run and heavily funded presidential campaign can get someone elected, but proof of acceptance will only come later. And the best proof would be how soon would it happen again, 4, 24, or 240 years from now?

Many blacks and others have feared for Obama's life as a leading candidate or as the president of the United States. This is an expression and question of how much acceptance there will be for the first black president of the United States. Furthermore, if Clinton or Obama make reference to any disparities of treatment or voter tendencies and challenges because of gender or race, they are frequently accused of "playing the race card" or the "gender card." Such allegations will often cause the pioneer to retreat from making such points in the future. In political circles it has become a way to disarm pioneers and often causes them to be silent about making such insightful, sometimes courageous and necessary, points. All of these dynamics are just some of the components present in the black quarterback syndrome.

Dictionary definitions describe a syndrome as a group of characteristics and symptoms that occur to create a condition. A number of the characteristics and symptoms, and resulting conditions that make up BQS have been described in this chapter. The examples that follow are a variety of specific comments, phrases, or thoughts that can lead individuals to experience the questions, doubt, and lack of confidence that often accompanies BQS and signal that the syndrome is "in play." Although not always intended to be so, often these comments are oppressive and persistent. Minimally, they can drain an individual's energy.

Examples of the Black Quarterback Syndrome Being in Play

Pertaining to the football black quarterback

He is a good scrambler but can he pass from the pocket?

He keeps leaving the pocket because he prefers to run.

Can he read the defenses well enough?

How long will it take him to learn to read defenses?

He's a gifted athlete but are his passes accurate enough?

He is a good scrambler but …

Will white players follow his leadership?

How long will it take him to learn the offense?

Does this person have the confidence to run this team?

Try him at running back.

Blacks don't play quarterback

Move him out of the quarterback drill line and over to the running back line.

Pertaining to Senator Barack Obama as a presidential candidate

He's not black enough.

Why won't he wear the American flag pin?

You know he is a Muslim.

He's the first "clean" African American candidate.

They are going to have to change the name of the White House if Obama is elected.

Rush Limbaugh referred to Senator Obama as a "Halfrican American."

He keeps talking down to black people — Jesse Jackson comment in response to an Obama speech.

<u>Pertaining to Senator Hillary Clinton as a presidential candidate</u>
She's the queen of pantsuits.
She's like your ex-wife.
She is Hillary the Nutcracker.
Iron my shirt.
The reason Hillary may be the front runner for Democratic Presidential candidate is the sympathy of women because of Bill's exploits.

Varying Degrees of the Black Quarterback Syndrome

All black quarterbacks in business organizations, just like black quarterbacks in the NFL, are not affected to the same degree by BQS. The reasons vary but can generally be attributed to the individual's sense of self, his or her self-confidence, personality, previous experiences, and current organizational support. One of the most important factors is the kind of organizational support that results in the employee feeling welcomed and belonging the entire time they are in the organization…not just the first week! The individual performer who is easily hurt or wounded when a superior gives performance feedback will struggle through BQS. The performer who is mentally secure, has the knowledge, skills, and ability for the position, expects various job challenges but feels deeply able to simply glide over any hurdles will no doubt experience less BQS turbulence. Conversely, performers with those same individual characteristics but who face the circumstances of an insensitive organizational culture, poor management, and organizational support——who doubt their capabilities because they look different——will face strong currents from the black quarterback syndrome.

Who will and won't succeed when faced with the syndrome's symptoms? Questions to consider include: how much of an impact navigating the BQS will have on the individuals, team, environment, customers, and organization? The placement of performers or black quarterbacks in situations in which they can succeed becomes an organizational necessity for the business that wants to out-compete and win over the competition. Today's organizations must be nimble and move quickly, be able to dance like elks not elephants. Organizations cannot afford to have leaders, managers, and executives mired in the black quarterback syndrome.

Marlin Briscoe wrote of his suspicion that having grown up sports-wise in a mostly white environment in South Omaha, Nebraska, and having played at a mainly white college helped him assimilate in his first black quarterback NFL role. Fortunately, he found support to sustain him in each circumstance. He also believed that some of the black quarterbacks that followed him into the NFL but who came from black colleges and probably all-black life experiences before joining the NFL, experienced more adjustment problems than he did. That seems reasonable and logical and, once identified, such adjustment problems can be solved and managed. The key is to have the awareness of the problem and the knowledge of how to solve it. That, in essence, is why I have written this book. What are solutions that we all can use in the future should we find ourselves being a "black quarterback," being a team member to a black quarterback, or simply being an observer or witness of such circumstances?

I should also point out that there are a number of pioneering individuals who will not experience the black quarterback syndrome. They may have particularly strong adaptation skills, or unusually strong supportive team members, management, or support systems that blend so well together that the individual's orientation and transition takes place smoothly and rapidly. In these instances, time, energy, and emotions are preserved for constructive production and doing the job. Senator Barack Obama was an example of a pioneer or "first" who did not appear to suffer from BQS. While Senator Obama was the first black individual elected by the Democratic Party as the presidential candidate and now has become the 44th president of the United States, he does not appear to be, judging by his own behavior, a victim of the black quarterback syndrome. Yet, he may daily face the syndrome. While at Harvard Law School, Obama was the first black person to head the Harvard Law Review. He no doubt had a list of other pioneering accomplishments. His confidence, poise, and determination remained strong. While people around Barack Obama may have put in play elements of BQS, the man himself did not blink or appear to fall victim to self-doubt or performance failure.

It should be obvious that progressive organizations would want their pioneering employees to avoid the black quarterback syndrome entirely or to help them find a way out of it as quickly as possible. Certainly this would be the aim of organizations seeking to be the most competitive in their particular business environment. When employees perform below their job experience or educational level it is both draining and a critical waste of time. Therefore, the issue is to avoid having anyone — manager, leader, executive — experience the black quarterback syndrome, but how to accomplish this? To find out, let us look at the meaning of being first and at some of its challenges.

"I can live for two months on a good compliment."
Mark Twain

Chapter 2
Pioneer's Challenges and Earning Respect

The Challenges

Being a "first" or a pioneer is like performing on stage in a theater, only this theater is your workplace. And though your co-workers are on stage with you, as a pioneer, the spotlight is often on you.

Put another way, think of the pioneer's co-workers as part of the theater audience watching a highly advertised play. Like most of us, they will reserve their evaluation until they are able to determine how good it is for themselves. Many times, they become more critic than spectator. It's not that they are against watching a good play; in fact they might prefer it to be good. And if the play is somewhat pioneering in nature, they might even be skeptical. But since it would not be fair, objective, or politically correct to admit to such bias they don't admit it to others...or themselves. There are various forms of this scenario that the pioneering employees will face with their audiences.

Many pioneers will argue that only those who have walked in their shoes, been their age, color, religion or ethnicity, will come close to understanding their particular challenges. Perhaps this is true, but it begs the question of how much cultural, social, or other background does one need to know to be a co-worker of someone who is a pioneer and therefore potentially facing the black quarterback syndrome? That is a very complex question to answer. I think the more important pursuit is to understand that there are unique challenges for pioneers and that they will differ depending on their individual personalities, experiences to date, position level, and the employee relations and management environment in the organization. In considering these factors, let us look at a "List of Pioneer Challenges." It is impor-

tant not to judge whether you agree or disagree with

these challenges, but to understand that they are shared

by working people who have achieved significant-level

positions. Their organization levels could range from

supervisor to CEO in organizations that range from

List of Pioneer Challenges

1. Many doubt you since they have not seen someone like you in your position.
2. The doubts of others may become internalized in the mind of the pioneer employee.
3. Others may not be doubters, but they marvel at how different you are and continually send off signals and reactions that indicate how different you are as they work with you.
4. It is sometimes hard to make friends or form trusting relationships because the difference and the social distance that is present causes a strain for both others and yourself.
5. Sometimes customers have never seen anyone like you in the position.
6. Sometimes the geographic region may never have seen anyone like you in the position.
7. Management may have to decide whether the region or market is ready for you — or if it is even fair to expose you to such a challenge.
8. Even family, relatives, and friends can wonder why you want to do that work? "I never saw anyone like you do that — good luck though." Some don't even wish you luck; they just shake their heads and keep wondering.
9. There can be peer envy or feelings can arise in peers that they don't understand themselves. A peer might wonder how you can be so good while facing your pioneering challenges. They might resent that you are as good or perhaps better in your performance than they are, even though they don't face the challenges that you do.

10. You might wonder about things that happen that make you feel uncomfortable. Are they because of who you are?

11. When asking for help or to attend some form of training, you wonder if they will think it is because of your difference that you need extra help — you wonder if the majority of the staff would have asked for help.

12. When it is suggested that you consider personal development initiatives or even advanced development support endeavors, you wonder if it is because of who you are? Would this be done for everyone? Should you even care or concern yourself with these thoughts?

13. You constantly wonder about things and this could be emotionally draining, could interfere with how you behave. You wonder whether they are giving you this great support and training and asking you how it is going because they think you are slow, need extra help or some other reason that you are missing. Are they concerned for you or concerned that you can't do the job and are seeking the evidence?

14. There may be social distance brought on by gender, age, race, economic class, education – others may be unsure of how friendly or supportive to be. Also, they may just not have experience with others like you, so they may be more reserved toward you. The question is how should you evaluate or understand how they are. Will this make you feel frustrated, angry, unsure, lose confidence, okay or lonely.

15. It may be harder to network or be friendly with others on your level because of the differences and the disadvantage here is obvious.

16. Your interpersonal skills must match those of the corporate culture and the expectation of how people like you are generally seen or you may be wrongly labeled somehow because of this mismatch.

small to multinational.

Earning Respect

Receiving respect begins by understanding and appreciating your own value. So how do you obtain this? If you have a position that causes you to question whether you might be experiencing BQS, that alone should tell you something about how valuable and good you must be at what you do. You have significant responsibilities, must be fairly visible, and be periodically called upon to make important decisions that if incorrect would be costly to the organization. However, when all the work and challenges start coming at you, it becomes necessary to declare, suggest, demand, ask for, and insist upon the respect you deserve. This must, however, be done with poise, not anger or frustration. Learn to tell others how well you are doing and how well things are going. We feel obliged to let our superiors know when things go wrong. Well, be certain to tell when things are going right! Don't be shy but definitely don't be cross. Also, praise others when they do well, especially if they are your subordinates or are on your team. Co-workers or subordinates may never have been given the respect or praise they deserve. Emotional intelligence expert and author Robert Cooper cited in his work that a 1995 Center for Creative Leadership study reported that "58 to 93% of people at work feel they have never once been genuinely recognized by a manager or supervisor." So you see, you are likely to be exceptional if you give and share praise and respect.

Remember, too, that receiving respect has a lot to do with looking and acting like you should be given respect. Walk, speak, dress, move, and, indeed, act as though for anyone to do otherwise would be an insult. Be sure to speak and write in the active voice, the certain voice, and not a passive voice.

Furthermore, look around at the employees and management members who command respect. Observe how they carry themselves. For your part, always look into the eyes of people whenever you talk with them. Expect all assignments you make to be completed and delivered on time. And follow up on their status. Don't pretend you have forgotten. If staff members are late, look them in the eye, acknowledge the due date, and then ask "When can you deliver on this?" Co-workers expect this and when you don't uphold your end, your respect begins to erode with them. You can always grant an extension, but let them know you had an agreement and unless otherwise informed, you expected it to be upheld. You should do this in a sincere, respectful way because when you don't show respect, it is a certain way to lose it. Most of us know someone for whom we have lost respect because they treated others without respect or they made us think they don't really care about the work.

There is nothing like success for gaining respect. Although I have been a New York Yankee hater all my life, I give them tremendous respect. Most of us greatly respect Bill Gates, Oprah Winfrey, Tom Brokaw, and Jack Welch; whether or not we like them, we tend to respect their accomplishments. It follows that success is a generator of respect. This is frequently seen in sports where winning teams earn respect, even when there may be troublemakers and recalcitrant players in their midst. Part II of this book is entitled "The 12 Steps to Success for Pioneers." A thorough understanding of these will do much to help you combat BQS and succeed in your career.

"It's not the size of the dog in the fight, it's the size of the fight in the dog."
Mark Twain

Chapter 3

What Some Firsts and Pioneers Think

In addition to my own perspectives gleaned from having been a pioneer many times during my 41 years of professional work, I interviewed a variety of individuals with varied experiences. Those experiences ranged from having been the first Muslim and Pakistani in a medical residency program at a U.S. state university, to being among the first Jewish students at a small Catholic all-women's college in the 1930s, to being the only white male basketball player on an all-black basketball team in an inner city high school that, years before, had been all white. While the interview sample size was not large, the experiences reported were large and extremely valuable. I offer what these successful individuals thought could be helpful to one in the role of a pioneer in an organization. Their responses are condensed and summarized on the interview questionnaire (the same questionnaire was used for all of the interviews). The results indicate that the majority of the interviewees shared a core of reasonably similar opinions.

"

Interview Questionnaire for Pioneers

Question 1. Were there special challenges to being a first or pioneer? If so, what were they?

Summarized responses:

Often I could see the look of interest, puzzlement, curiosity, or wonder, on the faces of some people at work, including managers and co-workers.

It was important to bring my family on board for support because on occasion they didn't understand why I wanted to put myself in such a new and potentially demanding situation.

You have to work to be two, three, or four times better than others to prove yourself. That is simply how it is when you are a pioneer. It comes with the territory and if you don't work hard and do well, you can blow the opportunities for others like yourself in the future.

Being left to sink or swim can be painful and produce doubt. Of course, there can be doubt in the eyes of co-workers and managers too, simply because you are a first.

There can also be periodic times or questions or doubt within yourself as you try to learn and perform your position.

All of these challenges sometimes became tiring and I wondered about ways to find relief.

Often there was no one to speak with about these feelings and I could occasionally feel pretty lonely.

Question 2. Did the challenges turn out to be the same or different than what you had imagined before beginning the job? If so, how?

Summarized responses:

Some were surprised that the challenges were worse than expected.

Some were given preparation on what challenges to expect by caring associates, family members, or even teachers, and in those instances were not surprised by the types and degrees of challenges.

Some expressed frustration because on occasion they were made to feel by others that, despite being comparably competent to others, they were Affirmative Action hires. That is, in the view of some, the primary reason they were hired or promoted into the position was to comply with Affirmative Action laws or bring diversity into the organization. It was challenging to have my competence questioned and obscured by whispers that I was hired because of Affirmative Action and not my knowledge skills and abilities.

Question 3. How did you overcome the challenges of or barriers to being a first?

Summarized responses:

The best way to overcome the challenges and barriers

was to be the best that anyone had ever seen do the work, trying to be much better than anyone else.

You might not become the best, but you had to strive for that anyway.

Study, prepare, go to training, and keep your eyes open to learn what behavior, knowledge skills, and abilities were most valued.

You didn't give up, because you must stay determined and on course.

You always self-assessed how you were doing and adapted when necessary.

You had to be patient and sometimes you had to put up with some tough circumstances.

Sometimes you had to stand up for yourself and explain or describe what might be unfair from your perspective and explain why. Your explanations had to be backed up with facts, reasons, and objective reporting or it meant you were taking an even greater risk by speaking up. You might be seen as whining.

You needed to always remember that you were there to do a job, not celebrate that you were a first or pioneer.

Question 4. How would you advise anyone to overcome the challenges of or barriers to being a first?

Summarized responses:

Be grounded and surround yourself with mentors both in the organization and outside of it.

You must really believe in yourself.

Immediately clarify what the expectations are for the position in which you are to perform.

You must have principles, religious or otherwise, so that when things get rough, you have them to help sustain yourself.

You will recognize that you have to be very competent, but try not to absorb negative feedback in a personal way.

Understand the importance of and relationship of PIE (Performance, Image, and Exposure) to yourself.

You must be seen as among the best and you cannot be average.

Understand that you are not the first to do this...understand that, "when you are a first you are an original and that the original is better than a wanna be."

Know that the bosses do not smile all the time and have their pressures, too.

Find out what the superiors' pressures are and try to help relieve some of them.

Try not to let the pressures of being a pioneer wear you down so that you will divert from your plans and the big picture.

Understand that there are external pressures and internal pressures and that you put your internal pressures on yourself and sometimes without evidence that there is even something to be concerned about or that there is a problem.

Let go of being a pioneer; don't think constantly about being one because it can wear you down.

Be very cautious about attributing adverse events or things that happen to you as being tied to being a pioneer.

Learn to fit in and be good at what you do.

Use the skills that got you there to overcome adversity.

Find allies in the organization and know that often there can be fantastic allies. Too many times possible allies are overlooked.

Invest in and develop others; it often comes back in good ways and results.

Strive to be socially competent and comfortable. Much information can be obtained and learned from engaging with others socially.

Go to the social events, even when your wife, husband, boyfriend, or girlfriend would prefer not to go!

The social gathering may not provide your favorite food, your favorite music, or favorite social setting, but it can provide information and improved relationships and new relationships...so go. When you don't go, understand that others will be gaining an advantage over you.

Find safe havens for yourself, family, friends, and others. Surround yourself with positive thinkers, people who have a light in their spiritual souls!

Question 5. Do you see any advantages to being a first or pioneer? If so, what might they be?

Summarized responses:

There can be advantages because you are noticed quickly and if you are really good and evaluated fairly, you hope it will be recognized and remembered.

On occasion the expectations of others about you as a pioneer are so low, it is easy to surpass their expectations.

Often, when you are a pioneer, you see things differently in instances where new vantage points and new thinking are necessary. When you can sell your view, it becomes an advantage for you and the organization. You can be seen as having new and fresh perspectives in some organizations (not in all organizations, unfortunately).

You can also give yourself some points for being a pioneer and that can be personally rewarding and motivating if you want to help others like yourself.

Being a pioneer can give an individual leverage or powerful influence when trying to bring other competent pioneers along with your own success.

Being a first is a record that cannot be broken because there is no one before you. Therefore, some individuals might glean some personal satisfaction from this position.

Question 6. What else would you like to say, given your understanding of the topic and considering questions that I may not have asked?

Summarized responses:

It takes a lot of personal understanding to break stereotypes as a pioneer.

Sometimes it takes family unity and parental guidance and preparation, particularly at a young age, to have the security and strength necessary to become a pioneer.

The demands of a pioneer to perform at such a high level can take the pioneer away from the family, so it helps to have family support and understanding.

The pioneer may have to give the family explanations about the nature of the position in order to get understanding and support from them.

There are support groups for various individuals who may be pioneers, so find them and use them to help become more skilled and to make life easier.

Do not become overwhelmed by the reality that you are a pioneer and let nothing stop you as long as you know that you are very competent.

Learn what causes you tension and what about yourself might cause tension in others and work to reduce this when it is appropriate.

Appreciate that having cleared a path for others is not only satisfying but noble work.

Maintain and demonstrate absolute integrity — you must not lose the trust of people!

Recognize that you have been blessed to be where you are in life compared to others like yourself who may have run into detours.

Remember that when you have problems, it is not always because you are a first or pioneer. We sometimes find that there are jerks in the workplace.

Remember, if you focus on being first, you are focused on yourself and not the work that needs to be done! Be careful!

"Snapshots" of 20 Interviewees

Below are the names of the 20 individuals who were interviewed for their insights about being a first or pioneer. After each name is a brief description of what made them a pioneer and often what happened in the future:

Ruth Alpert, a 1936 graduate of an all women's catholic school, Albertus Magnus College, in New Haven, Connecticut, was one of the school's first Jewish coeds. After graduation from Albertus, when the tuition was $450 a year, Ruth started her career at Yale University, where she worked in various positions, one as a lab technician. In 1972, Albertus Magnus College went coeducational.

M. Saud Anwar, M.D., of Hartford, Connecticut, is an internist with specialties in pulmonary and critical care medicine. He was the first Pakistani and Muslim resident at the University of Illinois, Peoria. Also, since his residency, he has been a first and pioneer in other medical organizations. Dr. Anwar was recognized by the American Red Cross after the 9-11 disaster in 2001 for his role in helping and coordinating a network of physicians in Connecticut, New York, and New Jersey to give support to affected families.

Marlin Briscoe was the first black starting quarterback in the National Football League (NFL). He is author of the book, *The First Black Quarterback,* which affirmed the concept of this book and led to it. Briscoe was a member of the 1972 undefeated Super Bowl Champion Miami Dolphins. A screenplay for a movie has been written about his journey to become a quarterback. Readers of this book should be on the alert for its eventual debut. For more information on the movie, see: *http://www.marlinbriscoemovie.com*

Dr. L.I. Diuguid, Ph.D., a 91-year-old black scientist, earned his Ph.D. in Organic Chemistry from Cornell University in 1945. Unable to gain employment with dignity in a chemistry job, despite a Ph.D. and a degree in education, Dr. Diuguid started his own laboratory and manufacturing plant in 1948. As a first black scientist and manufacturer of various consumer products, Dr. Diuguid experienced blatant racism in seeking to sell his researched, developed, and manufactured products in the marketplace. Dr. Diuguid still owns and operates his business, the Du-Good Chemical Laboratory and Manufacturers in St. Louis, Missouri.

Lewis Diuguid, who is now vice president for Community Resources of the Kansas City Star, was the first black person named to be bureau chief and then-vice president at the Kansas City Star. Lewis has received more than 60 awards, including the Missouri Honor Medal for Distinguished Service in Journalism and the 2007 University of Missouri Faculty Alumni Award. He is the son of scientist Dr. L.I. Diuguid of St. Louis.

Norman Elliott, M.D., is a practicing physician in Atlanta, Georgia, with a specialty in gastroenterology and internal medicine. He became the first black board member of Emory Health Care and was also the first black Assistant Adjutant General in the Alabama Air National Guard. Dr. Elliott retired in 2008 with the rank of Brigadier General. Additionally, Dr. Elliott remains active as the first black chief physician of the Atlanta Braves baseball team.

Hallie Gregory, Ph.D., became the first black high school coach in the state of South Dakota in 1962. Doctor Gregory also became the first black coach at Minnesota State University, Moorhead (formerly Moorhead State University) and eventually became the first civilian as well as black coach/first teacher/first administrator at the United States Coast Guard Academy in 1971.

Mark Grove had the unique pioneering experience of being the only white player on the otherwise all-black basketball team at James Hillhouse High School in inner city New Haven, Connecticut, in 1969 and 1970. Mark experienced many of the same kind of indignities that blacks experienced when they were pioneers in organizations. After positions in corporate America, Mark founded his own business, Career Conferences of America, which enabled college graduates who attended his job conferences to find jobs with many of the best companies in America. He would eventually specialize in matching minorities and women to appropriate organizations.

Jack Hasegawa, MTS, was one of few Asian Americans to take part in the 1960s civil rights movement and, interestingly, on occasions was made to feel that he should explain his presence in the movement as though it was only about whites and blacks. His presence in the civil rights movement was clearly supported by Dr. Martin Luther King's famous quote from the *Letter From Birmingham Jail*, "Injustice anywhere is a threat to justice everywhere." Hasegawa was the first Japanese American to become director of a major Yale organization, Dwight Hall. Currently, he is Bureau Chief, Office of Educational Equity, Connecticut State Department of Education where he is the first Japanese American to reach his position

Elmer Henderson Jr. was appointed the first black fire chief in Allingtown, CT, in 2001. Henderson had previously been a lieutenant in the New Haven, CT, fire department. Henderson retired in 2005 as chief and moved to North Carolina.

William A. Howe Ed. D., was the first Chinese American manager hired by the Connecticut Institute for the Blind

(1986); the first Chinese American manager hired by the Connecticut Department of Children and Families (1993); and the first Chinese American to achieve the level of Education Consultant in the Connecticut State Department of Education. Currently, he is an education consultant for the Connecticut State Department of Education, Bureau of Choice Programs.

Jimmy Jones has been the first black executive at a number of companies, the most recent being Reebok International, Ltd., where he was senior vice president and chief human resources administrative officer. He retired from Reebok in 2004 and is now president and CEO of Jimmy Jones & Associates, an international consulting organization that provides executive coaching and search, diversity and multiculturalism development, and world-class interim human resources leadership transition services.

Ruth E.G. King, Ed.D., an educational psychologist, has been a major consultant and trainer with organizations in the area of cultural diversity. Dr. King is also the author of three books. One, *The Only One*, is a novel whose heroine has a top level position at the Pentagon, and triumphs over gender discrimination and racism there. The book, while a novel, is laced with truthful experiences that the author has herself experienced or observed.

Donna Lopiano, Ph.D., the first woman athletic director at the University of Texas, was hired by its football coaching legend, Darrell Royal, in 1975. She served there as Director of Women's Athletics for 17 years. After leaving the University of Texas, she was Chief Executive Officer of the Women's Sports Foundation and has been named by *The Sporting News* as one of "The 100 Most Influential People in Sports." Lopiano is currently president of Sports Management Resources, a consulting group that helps educational institutions adapt to change in scholastic and collegiate athletic programs.

Timothy Ludwig, at the age of 24, became the youngest manager for the MONY Group, a northeast-based premier provider of financial services. He managed a group of 20 to 25 financial advisors, all of whom were considerably older than himself and some even old enough to be his father or mother.

Ludwig experienced the challenge of being seen as young, green, and, perhaps, inexperienced. At national sales meetings, the pressure of being taken seriously was magnified even more, as older and higher-level managers were in attendance competing for favor and improved career possibilities. Today, nearly 10 years later, Tim is district manager of his own financial services office, Charter Oak Insurance and Financial Services Company in New Haven, Connecticut.

Francisco Ortiz Jr. was the first Latino police chief in New Haven, Connecticut, as well as in the state of Connecticut. He started as a patrol officer and, during his 30 years on the New Haven Police force rose to become chief. Chief Ortiz is a national speaker and is sometimes sought for his opinion on the use of identification cards to help protect as well as integrate immigrants into the community. The chief retired from the New Haven Police Force in 2008 and became the Director of Public Security at Yale University's West Campus.

William Tong was the first Chinese American to serve in the General Assembly in Connecticut, having been elected in

2006. He was the first Asian American to be elected at the state level in all of Connecticut's recorded elective history. Representative Tong was the first Connecticut legislator to endorse Senator Obama for president of the United States. While at the University of Chicago Law School, Tong was a student of Barack Obama's and was inspired by Obama to enter public service. He was particularly moved by "the power of his (Obama's) vision for this country and our people."

Gale Richard was the first black laboratory technician hired into the consumer products division of Warner-Lambert, the pharmaceutical company He worked for Warner-Lambert for nearly 30 years in a variety of scientific, technical, and management positions in which he was a first or among the first. He left for other opportunities when the company was bought by Pfizer Pharmaceutical in 2000, moving to A.M. Todd, a manufacturing company in Michigan. There, he became the first black employee to achieve a management position, and there he remained until his retirement in July 2008.

Rosaida Rosario has often been the only Latin person on a number of predominantly white governing boards in the Greater Hartford region of Connecticut. Moreover, she is a founding principal in Rosario and Associates, a management consulting firm based in West Hartford, Connecticut. She has often been a pioneer, whether working for other organizations or in competing and selling her management consulting services to prospective clients, many of whom worked in predominantly white organizations.

Roberto Rosario, Rosaida's husband has often been the first Latino in a position or organization, most notably at Aetna Insurance Company, where he has spent the majority of his career in various management positions. As an associate in his wife's firm, he has shared with her many pioneering experiences.

"We ought never to do wrong when people are looking."
Mark Twain

Chapter 4

What Onlookers and Supporters of Pioneers Can Do

The Jackie Robinson and Pee Wee Reese Metaphor

"Laws control the lesser man...right conduct controls the greater." Mark Twain

The story of Jackie Robinson breaking the color barrier and becoming the first black major league baseball player in the modern era is well known. It is a story that is now taught to children at all levels in American public and private schools. There are biographical movies and books that present the oppressive acts, public policy barriers, and psychological challenges that Robinson faced on a daily basis in the course of a workday both on and off the field. It was 1947 when Robinson became a pioneer and integrated baseball for other black ball players as well as presenting the question for decades to come, of who is entitled to play baseball in America, which suggests who should be allowed to participate fully in American life? The answers to these questions had been evolving long before Robinson and 1947, but Robinson's place in American history remains extraordinarily significant and visible.

In America, we love our sports and in 1947, baseball was king among the sports we loved. Jackie Robinson's feat of surviving his painful role as a pioneer, a first, in baseball shone a light on the similar challenges that blacks and other groups faced when seeking employment opportunities. All of this is to say that Jackie Robinson's role as a pioneer is very much a metaphor for other pioneers or firsts who would follow Robinson, not just in sports, but, in the job markets, both for and not-for profit. An important piece of this history, however, is not as well known and that is the role played by the supporters of Jackie Robinson. Branch Rickey, the General Manager of the Brooklyn Dodgers, the major league team on which Robinson started, is given the most credit as a supporter of Robinson. Less well-known is the story of Pee Wee Reese. Pee Wee Reese was a white southerner already on the Dodger's team in

1947 when Robinson joined the team. Many players on opposing teams were against playing baseball with a black player and made it clear when the Dodgers visited their baseball parks. Even some of the Dodger teammates objected to playing with Robinson, thus adding even more pressure to Robinson's performance task. The fans at these ballparks were brutal in their taunts, death threats, jeers, and uncivil behavior toward Robinson. In one such tormenting moment in Cincinnati in May of 1947, Pee Wee Reese walked from his position at shortstop to Robinson at second base and put his arm around Jackie Robinson in a public show of support. This was a courageous and significant act and is mentioned as a pivotal event that helped Robinson decide to stay with the Dodgers. As a consequence, too, baseball players and fans begin to accept Jackie Robinson.

A bronze statue of Jackie Robinson with Pee Wee Reese's arm on Robinson's shoulder was erected outside of Keyspan Park in Brooklyn, New York. At the unveiling of the statue in 2005, Rachel Robinson, Jackie's widow, said that "Reese's gesture was proof that no one who stands up stands alone." These two men, a courageous athletic black baseball pioneer, and a courageous southern white man from Kentucky best represent the metaphor for this book, which is about how to survive in organizations as Jackie Robinson did, and, also why and how to be a Pee Wee Reese. Jackie Robinson and Pee Wee Reese were not disposed to complaining about how things were in 1947, but about "what to do and how to do it," as is this book in 2009. The next pages will speak to what onlookers and supporters who wish to emulate Pee Wee Reese can do to develop strong teams in the workplace where the Jackie Robinson-like pioneers perform.

What Onlookers and Supporters Can Do

"I was seldom able to see an opportunity until it had ceased to be one." Mark Twain

When firsts or pioneers are engaged in the work of their positions, there are usually other people working with, under, over, or tangentially to them. These individuals can be considered onlookers. Of course, they will also have an organizational role, such as being a director and a peer to the pioneer or a subordinate. It is of significant organizational value for these onlookers to have a sense of what challenges pioneers are faced with in their roles. However, since onlookers have their own role in the organization, it is legitimate to consider whether such situated employees should play an onlooker role. Will it conflict with or diminish their regular organizational role?

The fact is that for years organizations have functioned with individuals in management as well as nonmanagement playing the role of supporters for employees who are identified as being talented. In some organizations these people are described as being of "high potential"; colloquially, they are referred to as "high pots." The relationships that sometimes result in employees supporting other employees at lower, higher, or peer levels, have been widely accepted. There are a variety reasons that result in such roles. Often people just connect with each other. Graduates of the same college or individuals from the same part of the country may find a bond; sometimes it may be a hobby, a sport, or a mutual cultural interest. The business world, for example, recognizes that playing tennis or golf seals a lot of relationships. Mentoring, another example of such roles, is seen as being within company parameters and organizational policy. Mentors are often praised because they are useful in developing employees into superstars and high level executives, sometimes even the top leaders in a company. Mentors often rise to an even higher level of support called sponsorship. Sponsors are at a higher organizational level than the individual being promoted throughout the organization. All of this is to say that smart, effective onlookers are in position to be particularly helpful to the success of pioneers, so yes, being an active, positive onlooker is a legitimate organizational role for capable employees to take.

Some of the benefits that pioneers receive from being supported or sponsored are:

**Organizational information is shared with them.
**They can be informed of upcoming jobs or learning opportunities
**They can receive help in interpreting and clarifying their superior's expectations
**They can receive professional or personal coaching and counseling.
**They can receive personal information, tips, and collaborative assistance from them. (This is unlimited and open to a person's imagination; for example, financial and investment leads, social contacts, health tips, or religious counsel.)

Effective Onlookers Are Made, Most Are Not Born

How then does one become an effective onlooker — especially of pioneers? Should the organization encourage or even train onlookers to be effective? The answer is yes. In reality, being an effective onlooker is a form of teammate relationship. The team, of course, is the entire organization. Co-workers helping other co-workers to improve on behalf of the organization is a team-related activity. So how does the onlooker become an effective onlooker and not just a bystander, or worse, a negative force in the organization?

For starters, onlookers of pioneers might read and comprehend the first four chapters of this book to understand the nature of the challenges that the pioneer may be facing—that those are in addition to the position's requirements. Onlookers should consider how they might socially and emotionally support the pioneer. The first step is to try genuinely to know the pioneer. If this is not comfortable for the onlookers then they should examine and explore the reasons for discomfort. Incidentally, during hiring interviews, human resources people and management individuals should ask questions that enable them to hire people who are culturally competent and also cognizant and ethically caring of other employees. All employees should be encouraged to understand that they are all members of the same team. So, an employee becoming genuinely more familiar with co-workers should not be a stretch.

Vincent Messler, who was my boss more than 30 years ago at Connecticut Blue Cross and Blue Shield (now Anthem Blue Cross and Blue Shield of Connecticut), always had a way of making people feel that he was interested in them as a person, not just for the work they did for him. For example, he inquired about me, my graduate courses, and my life with interest. Even earlier in my career, when I reported to another superior who reported to him, I always felt Messler's interest in me—he shared much about his family, their vacations, his children, his volunteer work, and so forth. Years later, I remember a story of him parking the car in his driveway: his foot missed the break but hit the gas pedal, knocking one car into another, which resulted in the second car being pushed through the back wall of the garage. He had a smile on his face as he went on to say that he wrote a check for the repair work done, an amount that would have sent me into bankruptcy and depression. I recall thinking that I needed to save more money for such emergencies! Messler was the kind of person for whom relating to another was not a stretch. However, I have known many co-workers, superiors, and onlookers who would have had to stretch to express such genuine interest. Below is an article that I wrote to explain to recent college graduates how learning to stretch culturally and socially, can help them land their first job:

Diversity Stretching Can Help You Land That First Professional Job

If you are a college student seeking to be recruited into the professional workforce, one of the most important qualities employers will be searching for is your ability to be a "team player." For most employers this means working effectively with their experienced workers who in most cases are older than student recruits. It also means working effectively with employees who may be of a different race, religion, ethnicity, or socioeconomic group than you.

Performing well in a diverse work setting has become a significant employment issue since 1987 when the Hudson Institute published their Workforce 2000 report which made many projections of change in the composition of the U.S. workforce up through the year 2000 and beyond. The most striking change prediction and one that many found hard to believe was the sharp decline in the proportion of white males that would be new entrants into the workforce. The report projected that the traditional supply of white males would go from 47% in 1985 to only 15% of the new entrants into the workforce by the year 2000. The reality of those predictions has come true in many organizations at various levels and in parts of the country today.

Most reasonably progressive organizations have begun to address issues brought on by a more diverse workforce with various forms of diversity training. It is important to note that these organizations are not limited to either the Fortune 500 or private sector. Public organizations have begun to look at such issues as the effectiveness of their social, psychological, and other public services. In many instances, psychological treatment approaches and theories were developed with only white male clients in mind. This dilemma caused many social organizations to evaluate the effectiveness of their services and even to recognize that they excluded some diverse potential clients and markets. Given the competitive and economic challenges in the fight for survival faced by public organizations, this dilemma spotlighted new opportunities. Furthermore, the demand from excluded public sector markets and the need for quality service simply pointed out that failure to address this dilemma did not make sense. The importance of acquiring skills in valuing and managing diversity has revealed dilemmas of challenge, possibility, and opportunity in most businesses and organizations.

Neither have historically black colleges and universities (HCBUs) been exempted from diversity dilemmas and responsibility. Among the many virtues of HBCUs is to provide caring support and nurturing to black students who often report these ingredients missing from their experience at white colleges. The HBCUs now face the irony and challenge of convincing black students that they must learn to value and manage diversity. While black students seem ready for any challenge that will improve their chances for landing jobs and experiencing previously denied successful career opportunities; there is not an abundance of diversity courses available on the HBCU's campuses.

So the challenge for all college students is to understand not only the ethical reasons, but also the business reasons, for valuing and managing diversity in preparation for work. They must understand and believe that it can impact communications, teamwork, individual creativity, leadership capability, trust, loyalty, and, therefore, overall organizational effectiveness. As the private and public sectors make gains in each of these areas through pressing their diversity initiatives, organizations can actually improve their productivity, quality, and other results through these efforts. The big question becomes how to get the most from these advantages.

While the preceding questions have hung over U.S. organizations, many have begun to look to colleges and universities to provide them with students who are more culturally aware and capable of participating in and leading a diverse workforce. The "high flyer" white male who works well only with "guys" like his fraternity brother, will be a smaller proportion of the entrants into the workforce and may not be hotly recruited by the wise organization of the future. Yet, the white male who can work well with anyone will continue to be a premium value to an organization.

Colleges and universities can give students a decided advantage by helping them to be ready for the diverse workforce of the 21st century. Students perform well in job interviews and get off to quick, confident starts on new jobs when they have had some personal understanding and experience with people who are different from themselves. This is true for all aged individuals whether their difference is age, race, gender, ethnicity, religion, ability, organizational status or professional differences. Fortunately for employers, business schools and undergraduate schools have begun to seriously address these issues.

There are some specific things the enlightened ambitious student will want to do on their own or with help from their college or university. These things can make a difference in the effectiveness they experience during their adult working life. Let's call these things "personal stretching tips." Think of yourself as a large rubber band. The fact is that the more elasticity you have the greater the number of functions you are able to perform as a rubber band. Other rubber bands (young workers) may be the same size; however, they may have very little elasticity. When these human rubber bands are asked to stretch they might fray emotionally or even snap. Individuals who lack exposure to diversity or who fear diversity are often this way. They are tight when they come in contact with differences or diversity. Here are some of my personal stretching tips:

1.The next time you are at a reception or an event, force yourself to spend time with people you may normally avoid (Admit it, most of us do this — although often unconsciously). This may mean talking with older people, older men, blacks, whites, Latinos, Asians, a person in a wheelchair, whomever. Have some topics and questions in mind to discuss. The chances are good that they seldom talk with people like you and would find it interesting. Each of you might even learn something.

2. Ask yourself what groups of people you think you are superior to (Yes, I know you don't think that way and neither does anyone else!). The next time you talk with people from that group, keep good eye contact and listen intently to what they have to say as if it might change your life – and it might. Do the same thing with groups that you may feel are superior to you. (Examples of such groups might be people with graduate degrees, the faculty, certain majors, people from the suburbs, people from the city, athletes, nonathletes, the Greeks, the polo team, the poor, the wealthy, and so forth.)

3. The next time you have a chance, place yourself in a situation where you are the only one there like yourself or only one of a few. Examine how you feel and what you can do to make yourself feel more comfortable. And repeat this exercise at least twice a year. Examine any insights you gain as well as any growth in comfort from one experience to the next.

4. Occasionally skim newspaper and magazine articles that talk about people and cultures that are different

from you and your culture. Imagine what it would be like to work with them on a team or for you to work for them or have them work for you.

5. When watching television, wear reality lenses and remember that most groups and their characteristics, even the ones to which you belong are often exaggerated.

Applying the Golden Rule

Onlookers should watch and listen for opportunities to support pioneers. Many onlookers, of course, will not do this unless they believe there is value to the organization or to themselves. Fortunately, there are some employees — but they are exceptions, the Pee Wee Reeses, and Vincent Messlers — who are caring and considerate, and would seek to do this because they live by the Golden Rule, "Do unto others as you would have them do unto you." Many pioneers, unfortunately, have worked with too few Pee Wee Reeses. To be a Pee Wee Reese, it takes considerable courage, empathy, and understanding of the sometimes fragile nature of being human. Often there is tension in the onlookers that their expressed interest in the pioneer

88

may not be welcome. But isn't that what we consider in other relationships? Isn't the expression of interest in another the way that many of our best relationships began? So why let the fact, for instance, that the pioneer is the first Asian lawyer hired into the law department be an automatic reason for keeping your distance and not extending yourself? Or, why let the fact that the new analyst in your department happens to be a first Muslim who wears hijab dress, be an automatic reason for keeping your distance and not extending yourself?

Pioneers simply want to do their jobs and feel like they belong. Onlookers who are genuinely sociable with pioneers will help firsts feel as though they belong. Their actions will go a long way toward helping the pioneer give the organization the best he or she has to offer and also to succeed personally.

"Never put off till tomorrow what you can do day after tomorrow just as well."
Mark Twain

Chapter 5

What Organizations Can Do to Support Firsts and Pioneers

People who study and assess organizations often speak of their infrastructure. In doing so they are usually talking about the systems, equipment, policies, and even those things that support getting their products or services out the door, the value chain. When considering the product value chain, they are actually doing an internal analysis of the strengths and weaknesses of the organization. Decision makers take a close look at such things as operations, logistics, technological development, marketing and sales, procurement, and human resource management.

Yes, human resource departments are a link in the organizational value chain. After years of various challenges to Affirmative Action, the conservative tide that has, in the past, spoken against Affirmative Action has resulted in some members of human resource management becoming hesitant about strongly supporting Affirmative Action. Some have become reluctant to acknowledge openly that a recent promotion resulted in an employee becoming, for example the very first Latina, manager in the financial division...it just feels too sensitive and, therefore, is not discussed. It is what I call undiscussable and since it is undiscussable, important human resource components are certainly not going to have a strong place in the value chain. How, then is the pioneer going to receive the kind of organizational support that is given to other organizational elements? Yet organizations like to say, "Our people are the most important part of who we are or what we do." If they mean it, they need to provide support for their firsts and pioneers to insure their success.

Organizations have numerous systems designed to support their employees. They are referenced by such names as employee assistance, training, employee development, employee relations, flexible workforce, wellness programs, and managing and valuing diversity. Whether viewing these programs singularly or all together, their combined objectives are to enable the employees to be the best that they can be so that the organization can operate at its optimal level and be the best it can be. Yet, most organizations, because of sensitivities I have described earlier in this book, do not openly acknowledge firsts or pioneers by providing them with clearly targeted support based on their pioneer status. These organizations need to find an effective means to support their pioneers in a way that fits both their needs and the organizational culture. One way to do this is to relate such efforts to building what organizational experts refer to as a "learning organization."

What Is the Fifth Discipline?

Peter Senge, a Massachusetts Institute of Technology (MIT) professor, introduced the business world to the concept of the "learning organization" in his book, *The Fifth Discipline*. Senge is generally seen as the management guru who popularized the term, but many organizational theorists as well as leaders and managers have embraced the concept. A number of organizational presidents and their upper management officers have been trying to build learning organizations since the concept was introduced. Senge described what he meant by learning organizations in *The Fifth Discipline* as "organizations where people continually expand their capacity to create the results they truly desire, where new and expansive patterns of thinking are nurtured, where collective aspiration is set free, and where people are continually learning how to learn together." This means that organizations should be involved not only in building learning organizations, but in helping employees learn from each other and also how that can be done. There is much room to learn on behalf of firsts and pioneers as well as from them. What should be learned on behalf of the firsts and pioneers are the kinds of challenges and strategies I have mentioned earlier. Key among those points is that organizational management should understand that any employees could find themselves at some time experiencing the black quarterback syndrome. All they need to do is be different and find that they are the firsts.

I have already pointed out (see the interviews in chapter 3) what can be learned from firsts and pioneers. If the organization develops and sustains a safe and open environment, organizational members will learn far more than what I have already discussed. The information will be even more revealing because it will be the experiences of the employee in the organizational culture and structure that produced the black quarterback syndrome for that individual. Creating and sustaining an open learning environment that can produce such frankness can only come from a committed leadership within that organization.

An organization with a committed senior leadership must have a shared vision of the challenges of firsts and pioneers. Additionally, and equally as important, the leadership must have a shared vision and understanding of the definition of a learning organization. That definition should become the constant reference point, script, or playbook from which the organization designs, develops, educates, and communicates its vision for developing and sustaining a learning organization. Understanding the black quarterback syndrome, the role of onlookers, and educating organizational members about them simply becomes a by-product of creating and sustaining a learning organization.

In order to help your organizational management, its "black quarterbacks," firsts, pioneers, and all employees move toward becoming a learning organization, I recommend the following enhancement ideas set forth in a section of Peter Senge's *The Fifth Discipline Fieldbook, Strategies and Tools for Building A Learning Organization.*

" In a learning organization …

a. People feel they're doing something that matters — to them personally and to the larger world.
b. Every individual in the organization is somehow stretching, growing, or enhancing his capacity to create.
c. People are more intelligent together than they are apart. If you want something really creative done, you ask a team to do it—instead of sending one person off to do it on his or her own.

d. The organization continually becomes more aware of its underlying knowledge base—particularly the store of tacit, unarticulated knowledge in the hearts and minds of employees.

e. Visions of the direction of the enterprise emerge from all levels. The responsibility of top management is to manage the process whereby new emerging visions become shared visions.

f. Employees are invited to learn what is going on at every level of the organization, so they can understand how their actions influence others.

g. People feel free to inquire about each others' (and their own) assumptions and biases. There are few (if any) sacred cows or undiscussable subjects.

h. People treat each other as colleagues. There's a mutual respect and trust in the way they talk to each other, and work together, no matter what their positions may be.

i. People feel free to try experiments, take risks, and openly assess the results. No one is killed for making a mistake."

While all nine definitions provide for a comprehensive menu of learning organization definitions, d,f,g,h, and i are particularly strong definitions that support the concept of the black quarterback syndrome and how supporters and onlookers might behave.

Part II: Photographs

Author Norm Davis and first black NFL starting quarterback Marlin Briscoe after both spoke at Albertus Magnus College in 2004. Briscoe's topic was the challenge of becoming the first starting black quarterback in the NFL and Davis spoke about the black quarterback syndrome. Photo by Bob Hubbard

Displayed are Marlin Briscoe's book, *The First Black Quarterback* and Super Bowl Ring from that perfect season with the 1972 Miami Dolphins who were 17 and 0. Photo by Bob Hubbard

The author and 1936 alumna, Ruth Alpert, pose after class on *New Haven and the Problems of Urban Change.*

The author with Daniel Grove, Mark Grove and Marlin Briscoe after 2004 talk at Albertus Magnus College. Photo by Bob Hubbard

The statue of pioneer Jackie Robinson along with supporter and onlooker Pee Wee Reese. The statue stands in Key Span Park in Brooklyn and memorializes a significant day between the team-mates. The monument was crafted by noted sculptor William Behrenk of Tyron, North Carolina.

Part III: The 12 Steps to Success for Pioneers

Step 1

Starting a 90-Day Winning Plan

Start your success with a plan, a winning plan. I use "winning" to acknowledge that you are in a contest, yes, a competition against an insidious opponent — ignorance. The organization has never had someone like you in your important position. Uncertainty and even doubt may be a natural human response among others in the organization, both management and co-workers. Why? Because they simply have never before seen someone like you in this position. Imagine the pressure faced by the first woman school bus driver. There was a time when a pervasive, blatant, and insensitive stereotype existed that all women drivers drove poorly. Yet, today, one would hardly glance at a woman bus driver. And today, the day on which I outlined this section of the book, I delayed my writing so that I could watch at 8:06 AM EST, August 9, 2005, Colonel Eileen Collins land the Discovery space shuttle. Ten years earlier, Colonel Collins became the first woman pilot and commander of a shuttle mission. What a job she did and what pressure she must have felt landing the first shuttle mission since the Columbia accident in 2003. How much of the pressure would be attributable to the black quarterback syndrome — in this case, being a woman? I can't say and she may not acknowledge it at all. So many successful pioneers have learned to leave matters of race or gender out of the equation for how challenging their job might be. They fiercely protect themselves from being seen as whiners. This has been my observation for more than 40 years. Successful pioneers know the majority of people just don't want to hear about it, and if you do whine or speak of the BQS part of the challenge, they know there will be many people who won't see it and others who will even challenge the point. Whining highlights the interpersonal aspect of the challenge and diminishes the objective and vocational nature of what has been accomplished. The response might then be to label the person an angry or troubled individual, one who plays the race or gender card, or even something more demeaning. Consequently, pioneers like Eileen

Collins, Condaleeza Rice, and Colin Powell, prefer to keep the discussion on the job function nature of their challenge rather than on the racial or gender aspect.

Imagine the first woman department manager or vice president at a bank. Presumably, someone tells her what is expected and she understands. I say "presumably" because I know that sometimes expectations and objectives are not even communicated by the superior. The new pioneer manager, in this case a woman, should initiate her own 90-day winning plan that outlines the company's objectives for her position, steps that she should take to accomplish them, and her own specific benchmarks along the way. I suggest a 90-day plan to force her to avoid the risk of not recognizing missed objectives until the annual appraisal. Too much important time would be lost! The items in the plan may be finance-related, such as budget accomplishments, or relationship-related, such as gaining the trust of a rebellious subordinate. It is important to set a variety of objectives that will be accomplished during the first 90 days. Even if the objectives have been entirely accomplished, an assessment of progress can be made by this time. The following is an example of what might be a 90-day winning plan for this particular manager:

1. Obtain written objectives from my superior for the first year; coax them out of him/her if necessary.
2. Commence weekly staff meetings rather than the occasional ones held by my predecessor.
3. Meet with subordinates individually to assess what they each think our most important objectives should be. Ask them to Identify things we must do in order to be successful.
4. Understand and commit to memory the objectives identified.
5. Have my administrative assistant's position reviewed by the compensation department because I think it is undervalued and underpaid.
6. Complete a new marketing plan aimed at younger customers who don't have debit cards. Ultimate goal is to double the number of customers between 18–25 in

one year.

7. Get the entire staff to agree to the plan components for which they are responsible.

8. Speak with my organizational peers and selected others to obtain candid feedback on their view of the history and quality of our department's service to them.

9. Decide whether a new manager assimilation process is necessary at the end of the 90-day winning plan.

Of course, depending on the nature of the position, the circumstances of the hire, and other variables, you may have more or less items in your plan. Your objectives will also be different. Knowing your most important critical success factors and accomplishing them will help determine how you are seen and, in fact, contribute to a positive action-oriented reputation. Researchers say personal impressions are established within seconds of meeting someone. Michelle Sterling, an expert on image, impression, and impact, believes that within the first 3 seconds of a new encounter you have already made an impression and been judged. It is my observation that the majority of co-worker impressions are well established within 90 days of working with a new colleague and are very difficult to change.

Step 2

Claiming Victory From the Beginning

Beginning on the first day in your new assignment, talk in terms of your vision. If you do not have a vision, think about it and figure out what your vision might be. What is your mental picture of how you would like things to be with regard to your responsibilities, your position, and what it is that you are trying to accomplish. That is your vision. If your vision is different from the written vision for the department or unit, then you need to begin to resolve this difference. If you are a "manager" then you will be held responsible for your unit and will have to meet individually or with your team as a group to clarify what the vision is and should be. After all, you will be held responsible for carrying out the department objectives and they should support the vision so repair this disconnect as soon as possible. The good news is that you have become aware of the differing views of the vision. If you are not a manager, then your job is easier and it should just be a matter of talking with other team members and management to clarify what the vision is for the department or the function that you are fulfilling.

You do need to begin to speak from your vision as it applies to your position and the people who must support and/or work with you. Be sure that both subordinates and superiors understand and support your vision. Indeed, you should demand support for this vision from all of the collateral people involved as well. Keep sharing and clarifying your vision with others and always explain how it fits into the organization's vision. If you talk this way and act in this fashion, you will be seen as someone who understands the big picture and who can be trusted and utilized one day to continue building and preserving the business and the organization.

When you and your people act to support your responsibilities and vision, it is important to make this known to senior management. Claim your successes; describe how they were done, who contributed, what it does for the organization, and how eager you are to do more. If done confidently, yet tastefully, you won't be seen as bragging; rather it will be considered that you are sharing your results, sharing the progress being made. I find it necessary to mention that this is not bragging because when I have engaged in employee relations counseling with women and minority employees, many of them have reacted with discomfort at the notion that in addition to correcting their deficiencies, they should promote their successes. They understood and accepted the idea of deficiency correction, but their first reaction to promoting their successes was too often that their assets or positive attributes will be discovered and appreciated without their self-promotion. They believe they will be recognized, noticed, and valued simply because they are good. "Cream rises to the top" is the concept that they have learned to embrace. And I think the reason they are so initially committed to this concept is that they are extremely fair and objective. Pioneers receiving their opportunity are often quite optimistic and appreciative of their chance. They believe that this is how it should be and while it is how it should be, it simply is not the way it is. Are some performers so good that they don't need to engage in any self-promotion? Of course, there are some circumstances and environments in which this may be so; however, those are exceptional.

The vast majority of pioneers need to learn to practice self-promotion. The term "self-promotion" will be found in some management and organizational behavior books. You will also find the term "self-monitoring" in these books. Self-monitoring means to stay alert to correct and adjust to the situation or environment in which you are working. For example, if you arrive late to a meeting and notice that the boss raises his eyebrows, it may cause you to tell yourself that this will never happen again! If you are late to the next meeting, you are not good at self-monitoring. While most of us accept the concept of self-monitoring, too many of us are too slow to accept self-promotion.

Many successful people rise to the top by being comfortable with self-promoting — simply sharing what it is that they are doing right…and sharing what it is they are doing well…on behalf of the team and the organization. So get over it and practice self-promotion!

Step 3

Getting People to Stop Watching and Start Helping

The workplace sets up a competition of sorts and receiving help from the competitors and fans can sometimes rival a gymnast performing on a balance beam. When people accept new jobs or positions, especially the challenging ones, they all want to do well. We look forward to the day for us to start the new position! Looking toward the first day, no one thinks privately to him- or herself that, "I can't wait to start this new position so I can screw up and fail!" Yet the pioneer may be stepping right into a one-act play, or one-year tryout, with a dubious supporting cast.

It is often a curious event for the liberal, conservative, moderate, or nonpolitical person to discover that right at work they are engaging in something that touches United States public policies. The public policies that I am referring to are affirmative action, equal opportunity, and human rights…or just trying to be what is thought to be a progressive manager or employee. Suddenly it is noticed that we have hired a "first." A woman, a black, a Puerto Rican, an openly gay person, a person with a disability has been brought into the position. For some that makes work a little more interesting. Is this new person a token, an experiment, or a superstar? That makes for interesting viewing, even better than reality TV and far better than Trump's show, *The Apprentice*. After all, this is not 60 minutes of viewing, but daily viewing, and the co-worker might even decide to play a role in the drama. But, of course, since most co-workers want to be seen by other employees as fair and progressive, they presume to not notice that this is a "first" and just quietly watch the entertainment and observe whether the new hire can make it. If the pioneer's co-workers were asked about the pioneer's chances for success, they might question why he or she was hired, "How did Tyler or Mary get in here?" but finally proclaim, "I have nothing against this new person." Moreover, few co-workers express verbal support in favor of the pioneer because they are not sure if that would be politically correct. Yet the co-workers success is very often linked to that first or pioneer person's success.

So why should anyone help you, this new "first" person succeed? The answer is simple. Help and support each other for your own sake and that of the organization. It's all about relationships. I'm sure you've heard this before. But you may have doubted it or not made the most of the potential. Subordinates, superiors, collaterals, associates, teammates, friends, and others will not give each other help unless they have good relationships with each other. The question then becomes how to affect great relationships with others. This is done through careful listening and meeting the needs of co-workers. Your job, then, is to become a keen observer and discerner of the needs of those with whom you work. As an example, when you understand your subordinates' career plans and give them specific training, advice, insight, or opportunity, you begin to meet their needs and consequently develop better relationships. However, listening, observing, and perceiving must be among your most polished and perfected skills. Part of the listening function is the ability to wait until others have expressed their points of view before you react. These are important functional skills, critical to your success, for if help and support are lacking, you will be vulnerable to failure. Robert Cooper, an expert on emotional intelligence and leadership, and author of numerous management books, believes that "the most important leadership trait for winning in organizations is not having the best technology, products, or services. It's having the best relationships."

If, as a pioneer, you can meet a need of a co-worker, team member, vice president, or department manager, your relationship will change and, in fact, improve. For example, if you were to provide space, rare technical expertise, or extra labor support, or correct the delay in an overdue project, your relationship will improve with the person whom you have helped. Keep in mind that you must be perceptive in order to become aware of the need. Often people will tell you of their need and that makes it easier to determine whether or not you want to respond. Are you seen as a person who is likely to respond to such a requested need as well as someone who is also able to perceive the needs of others? If you are, you will have better relationships, and others will be more likely, if not eager, to help you in return.

So much of work — as well as of life — is about relationships. There are forces all around us leading to change. The forces nudge us forward, backward, and even into keeping the status quo. These forces reside in relationships. Strategic action plans, objectives, acquisitions, layoffs, mergers, new product creations, training, implementation of missions, and other organizational actions are all strongly dependent on relationships for success. And while everyone should want the pioneer to succeed for the sake of the organization, you may have to keep selling the importance of this. As a pioneer, keep offering your support and others will be grateful and never forget it. (Neither will they ever forget if you present hurdles for them to jump or obstacles for them to move.) Others will support you and even if they find themselves on the opposite side of an issue, their loyalty to you will cause them to explain clearly why they are not with you. That is fair enough; usually you can accept counter positions as long as you are given the courtesy of a clear explanation.

The most significant point here is that when you understand that work and careers are built upon strong positive relationships, then you will understand that "first" persons and most others will at some time be in position to support or help each other and you. Their help may be as little as speaking positively about you in a meeting in which you are not present or as big as asking you to apply for their job postings when they come up. Hopefully, the reader understands that much of what has been experienced in Step 3 applies not only to pioneers but to onlookers as well. Actually, it should be clear by now that these twelve steps and, indeed, the entire book can be adopted by anyone seeking to be successful.

Whether you are a pioneer, co-worker, or onlooker, if you are not building stronger relationships, you are building weaker ones. Why is this so? Because stronger relationships are being built by other people with each other while you are out of the picture. Those relationships are often constructed even if the individuals are not trying to do this. For example, two people who serve successfully on a committee together may subsequently experience a stronger relationship. Something as simple as two managers traveling together on a business trip can be a seed for a stronger relationship between these co-workers.

Those who are in the "first" or pioneering roles can benefit from some mutual stroking from well-earned relationships, enabling their seeds to grow and sprout. Is that so bad? The astute employee or member of management should easily see that benefit for pioneers and co-workers, and the payoff for the organization. No doubt you have heard the phrase, "If you are not part of the solution, then you are part of the problem."

Step 4

Understanding the Role of Social Competence and Comfort

The need to display good socials skills is a little known or seldom-discussed fact but it is a reality. It is assumed that one would not want to rise in an organization and face the pain of frequent exposure to constant interaction without having solid fundamental social skills. However, you know the line about making assumptions: they make an ass out of you and me (ass u me). Well, if you lack social skills, you will feel like an ass even if you choose to try to hide the fact. I've seen many a person who wondered why a move to the next level never happened. That level was significant and quite visible, but no one wanted to explain to the puzzled employee that the mediocre social skills were the reason. I know I never wanted to discuss social skills either when I first became a manager. The first few times I hinted to co-worker friends or even subordinates that they should polish their social skills, all I received was a blank stare, which was then followed by denial and comments about how strong they were with their technical skills. Alright, I thought, I don't look forward to raking up examples of how you seem painfully awkward when making simple introductions of one employee to another. Nor do I desire to line up witnesses to your social discomfort and lack of such skills, like a prosecutor facing a judge. Consider these points by imagining a manager informing someone that one-third of the office co-workers complain about that person's bad breath. The employee's response to this valuable and necessary information was to ask the manager to prove it, "Give me the day, time, and names of those who smelled my breath."

Informing employees of those personal and social "development opportunities" was a task that I learned to master in my employee relations manager role, but I never relished it. Fortunately, most employees accept social development feedback quite well. The problem is that, from the start, superiors often won't give this feedback. They think social skills feedback is off the table for performance discussion and find it too sensitive to engage in it. At times, when certain bits of feedback are given, you should just say "thank you" and begin your own survey to confirm or reject the data. Actually, employees would be smart to do their own social skills assessment without being asked. Just think about it. Are your social skills strong? Do they need improving? If so, which skills and where will you find the resources to improve?

Many managers find the need to improve social skills to be undiscussable. It is very important for employees to possess good social skills, particularly management level workers; it is like having good blood pressure and cholesterol levels. If you have them, you possess a healthy benefit that you don't notice and if you don't, it can quietly lead to death or the end of your career. The higher the individual rises in the organization, the more necessary it becomes to have strong social skills. The ability to socialize, speak well, and generally interact with all levels of employees has become so important that my college's business department, along with a number of others, provides role playing and mock cocktail parties and receptions to help prepare the students for their careers.

Underscoring still another aspect of the need for strong social skills is that management, administration, and the power people who make key decisions in organizations want to work with people with whom they are comfortable. They do not want to work with employees with whom they are uncomfortable. Very often socializing with each other increases the level of comfort. The activities that occur after work, off premises, can be the best ways to bond and increase comfort levels among employees. It is important for the pioneer employees to understand this. The pioneer employee should accept invitations to happy hours, cookouts, home visits, holiday parties, golf outings, and other social gatherings within reason. I clearly understand that often the pioneer employee will feel that these events are more like extending working hours than engaging in socializing.

One day, I hope, the employees who are in the majority will recognize the previous point and do at least the following:

> Consider that people who are "firsts" or who are in the minority in group circumstances, will feel much more comfortable if the majority group understands how to make them more comfortable and wants to, and, therefore, takes the initiative to do so.

In most organizations this topic is undiscussable and, quite frankly, the need for such a discussion is even denied. This denial is sometimes even shared by those who are "firsts." An employees is not likely to be frank with a boss and say "the reason I don't come to the Christmas party is my wife hates it and I don't like it either. We don't enjoy the music, food, or conversations with the other spouses and we constantly feel like it is just another form of work." I would love to see departments deal with the undiscussables associated with outside socializing and comfort. For now I will leave that to my own consulting work and a future book.

Employees increase their chances for success by having good social skills and a good appearance. Pioneer individuals can discern what appearance criteria exist by looking at the dress of others in the positions that they either hold or seek to attain. As a "first," dress reasonably similar to the way others dress who are doing what you want to be doing now and in the future. While I don't intend for this step to be a guide for professional etiquette, I can't help but reveal two subtle tips. First, I think it is important to display a confident firm handshake when meeting co-workers, clients and others. Second, do whatever it takes to look great in a white shirt or white blouse and wear this uniform frequently (this means keep control of your weight). By doing this, I think President Barack Obama disarmed a lot of people who ignorantly feared that his name and particularly his middle name (Hussein) meant that he might be an extremist Muslim. Yes, you can certainly entertain the question of how far you want to compromise. Keep in mind, however, that I have yet to see an American executive wear a kilt in a Fortune 500 organization.

Step 5

Bringing the Significant Others Aboard

Significant others are not the people in the organization with whom you have romantic relationships. Organizationally speaking, they are the key people in the organization whom you already know or should know. They are the people who have credibility, understand the business, understand the culture and how things work and why they work as they do. They have power and some of it may be from self-empowerment, because even though some may not have a very high-level position, people listen to them for their good ideas and opinions. You might even envy their charisma and influence. You might want to be like them. These are people with whom you need to become more familiar than the organizational structure will permit. The chain of command as well as each of your own responsibilities may keep you from having much contact, but you see them and hear about them occasionally. These individuals may not be on your team, or in your department, or even in your state or the country where you are currently working. Depending on your career vision and mission, you need to find out who they are and get to know these significant others. What you are looking to gain here is mutualism with them.

Organizational scholar and futurist Joel Barker, in his powerful video entitled, "Wealth, Innovation, and Diversity," speaks of mutualism as using our differences for the benefit of each other. In this case, I am suggesting that we use the education, department knowledge, organizational knowledge, as well as organizational influence of your significant others for mutual benefit. You want to engage in this commodity of mutualism with these significant other co-workers at any level you can achieve.

I know that this will be difficult if you are a level 3 supervisor and the significant other with whom you want to socialize is a level 8 vice president. Maybe in 5 years you will get to him or her and receive an invitation for golf. However, you can identify these people now and begin to socialize with those key people whom you can reach comfortably and immediately. Start by asking them to lunch, your treat, of course. Or invite them for a beverage after work. Invite them for a walk, tennis, golf, or a look at your rare stamps collection, but figure out how to become more familiar with them, perhaps through shared interests. Yes, offer them your resources…this is one of the ways that mutualism works.

During these periods of socializing and becoming more familiar, share your visions, your accomplishments, and your challenges. Seek the ideas, knowledge, and support of your significant others. Of course, this is networking but it is more aggressive networking with specific focus and direction. You should eventually ask for their support and offer yours to them. In time, you will find yourself being invited by those who like you and want your support and want to support you. You will come to be seen as someone who values the organization, understands its vision and mission, and understands that there is a bigger picture whose goals you embrace beyond your own personal career. Mission accomplished.

Step 6

Shaking Off the Unwanted Baggage Attached to Being a Pioneer

Usually there are stereotypes that accompany whatever characteristics make an individual a "first." When the employee owns the stereotype or accepts it, then it becomes that person's "baggage," or emotional weight. It is important for the "first" to resist and reject such stereotypes. Although it is psychologically difficult to reject all such stereotypes, it is important for "firsts" to learn to do so. Some "firsts" learn to do this on their own, naturally, or with the help of family, friends, and even therapy. The experiment done by Jane Elliott the third-grade classroom teacher in the classic Frontline video, "A Class Divided" (also known as "Blues Eyes and Brown Eyes"), demonstrates how challenging and disruptive the acceptance of stereotypes can be for an individual. In the video, Elliott first assigns negative stereotypes and places a cloth collar around the neck of the third graders who have brown eyes. Despite some minor resistance from the students, the brown-eyed students seem to accept the stereotypes. Elliott then makes the claim that brown-eyed students are not as smart as the blue-eyed kids, continuing to assign other negative stereotypes to the brown-eyed students. The brown-eyed children soon begin to exhibit drooping posture, act out in various anti-social behaviors, and perform below their previous levels of classroom work. Even the blue-eyed students began to accept that the teacher was correct in assigning the negative stereotypes to the brown-eyed students. The collar-clad, brown-eyed, disadvantaged or (out-group) students showed that people easily prefer being in the blue-eyed in-group. Very little support came from individuals in the in-group and hardly any resistance came from the out-group. Out-group behavior is typically characterized by a lack in confidence and negative feelings arising from identification with out-group stereotypes.

The challenge of being a "first" is to resist being a part of what could be seen as the out-group and at the same time to garner support from the often too passive and non-supportive in-group. In-group members often don't realize the advantage and privileges they possess and take them for granted as their right.

A way for those who are "firsts" to resist accepting stereotypes is to examine actual facts in association with a stereotype. A stereotype can usually be spotted when one thinks or speaks in terms of a characteristic applying to all people in a certain group. For example, that "all women" are bad drivers, and "all men" are sports fanatics. A quick research of the facts will reveal that neither stereotype is true for "all."

Pioneers must practice resistance and reject the stereotypes associated with what makes them pioneers. If the "first" happens to be the first Asian marketing director in the company, for example, he or she may be faced with stereotypes that come with being an Asian. Some of the undiscussed or unspoken stereotypes about Asians are that they are all exceedingly quiet and have poor interpersonal skills, and, therefore, cannot become good managers or leaders. That pioneer Asian director of marketing in XYZ Company might resist accepting those statements by addressing them one by one and determining that they are simply "not true!" With this recognition, the pioneer should go about work with the clear understanding that he or she was hired for the position and was thought to have the right qualifications. Further, if there might be any truth to those stereotypes (sometimes stereotypes are true), the pioneer should conclude that, in this case, those stereotypes do not apply and should be rejected.

Often, stereotypes are not easily resisted by those on whom they are projected. Additionally, the experience of being stereotyped, or observing others being stereotyped, can linger oppressively in the mind of an individual. Stanford University scholar Claude Steele coined a concept, "stereotype vulnerability," which illustrates an example of stereotypes being resisted but causing reactive or disruptive behaviors. Steele describes a condition in which blacks may behave in ways to avoid fitting a stereotype. In the following example, a black student may feel the need to sit in the front row of math class just to show the professor that all blacks do not sit in the back of the classroom. Obviously, this reveals a significant amount of thought about and preoccupation with the idea that others might be applying stereotypes. Keep in mind that any "first" can be stereotyped and, as a result, experience stereotype vulnerability.

When the weight of the baggage or stereotype is so heavy that the black student in the math class decides not to attend class regularly, the stereotype becomes dangerously harmful. In this case, imagine that the student believes the professor thinks all blacks are poor in math and lazy about work. This becomes an example of internalized oppression because the professor is not the one who is restricting the student. The student's own thoughts and beliefs are doing the job. Students who believe that a professor will not evaluate work fairly may decide not to make a committed effort.

This classic classroom example of internalized oppression can easily be related to a work situation. Consider that Marie, first woman manager in the mechanical engineering department for an aerospace company, assumes that the employees in her work group would prefer to work for a man. As a result, she does not delegate work or give much direction for fear that they will not want a woman to be their boss. Obviously her performance is hampered by her internalized oppression. There is no evidence that the men don't want her, but she restricts herself and holds herself down because of the stereotypical baggage that she is carrying with her.

There are other examples of stereotypes that a pioneer may experience. If, for example, someone is a pioneer because of race or gender, there is the possibility of being seen as an Affirmative Action promotion or hire—that the company hired the employee for compliance with Affirmative Action and not because of qualifications or skills. In this scenario, individuals constantly feel that their knowledge, skills, and abilities are under review by peers and others because, after all, they were Affirmative Action hires. There might be no mention of Affirmative Action by anyone, yet the assumption made by many could be that "it was probably an Affirmative Action hire."

Finally, women are often unfairly labeled with one or more stereotypes. They can be seen as too emotional, too detailed, too soft, too hard, too pretty, too dress conscious, too serious, and on and on. Add these stereotypes to the dynamic of being a first or pioneer and women approach the pressures of Marlin Briscoe facing the black quarterback syndrome.

Step 7

Claiming Victory Following the
90-Day Plan

If you have properly monitored your 90-day plan, you will have accomplishments to report on and share with co-workers, subordinates, superiors, and other appropriate people. Determine which accomplishments you should report and which vehicles you might use. Consider how others have reported their interim accomplishments and the culture of the division and company. Consider if you wish to be traditional in your reporting or would want to be bolder in sharing your early successes. Will you use newsletters, the grapevine, private conversations, meetings with the board, discussions with other managers, forums with the public, or releases to the newspapers to promote and share your early accomplishments?

At the same time, if there are shortfalls, do not avoid disclosing them to the appropriate people. Face shortfalls directly and inform the appropriate stakeholders that progress has been slower than expected. Explain why and describe the corrective actions undertaken in order to ultimately succeed. Explore whether to negotiate new deliverable dates or to examine the option of change in the due dates. If necessary, replace people on the project. Assess whether adequate resources have been committed, or whether some aspects need to be modified and whether to realign the deliverable components of the project.

Managing a shortfall that is corrected and then turns out to be a winner can be a major achievement for a pioneer. Follow-up on the 90-day plan should be done on schedule, with appropriate and fair-minded self-promotion of the successes and direct, energized confrontation of the shortfalls. At all cost, avoid last-minute surprise announcements that highly coveted results will not be met on time!

It is important to show comfort with detecting and correcting your own errors or shortfalls. You want to be seen as fearless and that things are genuinely going well most of the time, but that in the event of approaching problems, you will always confront them head on with practical and workable solutions. Further, it is important to convey that covering up a difficult problem, transferring it, or avoiding it are unacceptable options. Likewise, when performance is good and results follow, accept the credit for your staff as well as yourself. Share the success with others outside of your team when they have had a hand in it as well. The poet Madeline Bridges has said it correctly when she wrote, "Give the world the best you have, and the best will come back to you." Constantly share success and fight errors. Strive to have yourself and your people seen as those who detest predicting rain in favor of building arks! Indeed, proclaim that you are the ark builders and bailing-bucket makers!

Step 8

Building Your Business Network and Rewarding Supporters

After assessing your progress at the conclusion of the 90-day plan, you will have at least planted the seeds for developing some good relationships and a few may even have begun to sprout. More business relationships will develop as the time elapses and you grow into the functioning required in the position. A number of the relationships will be grounded in departmental affairs and others in social interactions and events that you have been building.

It is crucial that those co-worker relationships that are rooted in the interactional functioning of your position, in which people have supported you, your vision, and your areas of responsibilities, are rewarded or given recognition. Be generous if you have the resources to do so. Rewards may range from bonus recommendations, committee appointments, and taskforce recommendations to praise in business meetings or small token gifts. Create incentive programs to supplement creativity, teamwork, and supportive behavior. Budget for these items and consider them a necessary cost of doing business. If you or your department is seen as odd or different for doing this, so be it. Progressive companies and progressive managers have organizationally designed incentive programs for this. Do not make rewards automatic. They should only be given for recognition of identifiable and desired supportive behavior. The rewards should be carrots and dividends, as well as making payments for behaviors you would like to see repeated. Your own personal dividends will come through their continued support.

Your dividends will come in the recognition that even though you were a pioneer and you might even have done things in a slightly different way, your performance is being seen through eyes that assess your results and not what makes you different. That is all you are seeking. When this happens you will earn the security, promotions, assignments, opportunities, and respect you require and cherish.

A great way to add to the organizational network and reward others is to have a cocktail party that is really fun. Invite those who work under and close to you and consider how far-reaching you want to extend invitations. Have a purpose in mind for the party and if possible have it at home. The purpose could be to impress superior management, stimulate bonding opportunities among your staff and the people with whom you work most closely or even with another department. Keep in mind that those who don't attend your party or are not even invited will see that you plan to be a serious team player.

A few things to consider when planning the party are how many to invite, the food, drinks, and fun.

Invitations — Consider your purpose to help determine how many and whom to invite. Of course the space in your home or party facility is also a central consideration.

Food — It is not necessary to provide for a full-course meal but a nice array of hors d'oeuvres and simple foods will suffice. Keep in mind, too, that many people are making healthy choices when eating, therefore some fruit, nuts, and crackers and cheese should always be nicely presented along with your other foods.

Drinks — It is smart to hire someone or ask a good friend to serve as bartender. The same is true when it comes to servers. If you don't have help with making the drinks and finger foods easily available, you will never have time to enjoy your party or accomplish any of your purposes for having the party by being able to schmooze with your guests. Don't overindulge in the drinks yourself, but more importantly, don't let anyone leave who might need a designated driver. Plenty of coffee, tea, water, and a volunteer driver are good complements to a fun evening.

Fun — Few people have enough fun in their lives these days so give the bonus of planned fun at your business cocktail party. Don't rely on the news, politics, or office talk to provide the color and tone for your party. Draw a party curve which starts slowly, making sure that every-one meets all invitees. Introductions are usually good enough. Spend 15 minutes on the Internet and you will have enough ample ice breakers (reinforcing introduc-tions) and sophisticated fun games to have your co-workers clamoring for your next party — well maybe you don't want that…but plan the game fun from the middle to the end and let things wind down a bit just before turn-ing on the bright lights that signal, "The Party's Over," played on your MP3 player of course. There are a num-ber of download versions that Googling the title will bring to you. I prefer the Nat King Cole version — speaking of sophistication! The absolute best planning advice I can give is to take the Nike approach and "Just Do It!"

Step 9

Linking Social and Business Contacts to Each Other

An often-overlooked practice, except among people in sales, is linking and sharing your social and business contacts with each other. Consider the potential of synergy and mutual exchange opportunities by simply sharing your professional contacts when appropriate and desirable. Often there will be people with whom you work and others whom you know, who, for many reasons, should meet each other. Give a little thought to how you can make it happen. For example, your doubles tennis partner, who works in another company and industry, may be able to help your information technology (IT) manager by sharing an opinion about a software product. This can be a very inexpensive endeavor, time being the only cost, yet sharing the evaluation of the software product could save thousands of dollars. By brokering a meeting, you could help your tennis partner's company and your own company's IT person. The kind of products being considered could be a mismatch, totally out of line, or they could be superior and a perfect match. Your tennis partner, who has used the product, can make all of this very clear and even provide useful data. The idea is to constantly look for ways to help your co-workers and the company, all of which make you more valuable and indispensable in the eyes of both.

As you continue to build these social and business relationships, you will actually be participating in the construction of your own "social networks." There will be professionals in a variety of fields and at various levels in their organizations with whom you can call, e-mail, or meet for dinner, coffee, or a beverage of your mutual choice. All of these people will represent your social network.

The incredibly rapid growth and use of personal computers for personal matters has facilitated an explosion of online social networks that connect people with business opportunities. Computers also enable people to easily build business profiles with information obtained from social networks. This kind of information has been particularly helpful in the financial services and insurance business. Actually, the uses of online social networking are only limited by your imagination. The beauty of social networking is that it makes it easy for people with similar interest to help each other. One online social network, *Ecademy.com*, is frequently used for the building of business contacts between people. *Ecademy.com* also can be used to advertise services and products that are needed or available. *LinkedIn.com* is another very popular social and business networking site. Both are free sites although *LinkedIn.com* does have some additional services that can be purchased. Social networks can be used creatively for solving business problems or even social or personal problems. A social network could be used to make contact with people in a niche market, or even make personal contact with individuals who have similar social interests, for example, playing either chess or tennis. Career networking can also be done through many of the social networks that are posted and easily reached by various search engines. These four key word phrases will get you started on your way to hours of networking sites from a Google search: MyWorkster, Monster, career coach, and career networking.

Is Networking Manipulative or Unethical?

Some individuals find stretching to become familiar with people they don't know very well, to be uncomfortable. They claim to feel disingenuous, insincere, phony, and sometimes, even dishonest. Perhaps you have wondered if people will respond to your interest in exchanging information at work. Will they really latch onto your clearly articulated vision, support you, accept your rewards, or will they see you as manipulative? Nonsense! Co-workers and management will not see you as manipulative because most organizational cultures embrace these activities. Certainly, organizations that want to be progressive, embrace, if not sponsor, networking in some way such as management clubs, golf outings, or career clubs.

I remind you of the old spoils system and the current capitalistic system under which the United States operates. The spoils system means giving appointed offices and jobs to as many loyal persons as possible in the party that is in power. Historians believe that the system was so named from a speech in which Senator William Learned Marcy stated that "to the victor go the spoils." Presidents Thomas Jefferson and Andrew Jackson were early practitioners of the spoils system. The system became entrenched in state politics and is practiced on a national scale to varying degrees. How much still exists today is speculative because many practioners deny its presence and fear voter retaliation if they were to admit participating. The use of public offices for rewards for political party work is simply part of our economic culture.

Move this discussion of economic culture to an examination of economic systems and the most dominant system we see in the world today is capitalism. The earliest forms of capitalism had their roots in mercantilism and sprang from Rome, the Middle East, and also Europe in the early Middle Ages. The distribution of goods for profit became known as mercantilism. Mercantilism eventually grew into the economic practices that became known as capitalism. An examination of two fundamental characteristics of capitalism will be organizationally reminiscent in most corporations. First, accumulating capital, such as land, production tools, and materials, to then sell at higher prices is one characteristic. Today, in the age of technology, information and service must be added to the list of capital. Information can be sold, it can be used to generate business and organizational advantages, solve problems and numerous other things that a creative mind can envision. The exchange of rewards for support and information within our organizations suddenly seems quite natural.

The second fundamental characteristic of capitalism is thinking individualistically. People are different in our society and should pursue their own interests. Individuals and employees should be free to pursue their own economic freedom and this best assures the interest of society as a whole. Think progressively and understand that the large scale goal of capitalism is to produce wealth. Rewards given by the "first" or any employee in possession of resources, for information and support of their ideas and interest shows organizational savvy and appreciation. Networking is far from being manipulative or unethical. It is the right action for pioneers to take.

Step 10

Declaring Your Knowledge, Creativity, and Success

At this point you are past the 90-day plan and you have demonstrated your ability to detect and correct errors. You have sown seeds to garner support, you have offered support when possible, and, by now, should be seen less as a pioneer and more for who you are, what you have done and are doing, and how you carry yourself. You can encourage this view by speaking confidently, saying that you know what you are doing and reporting that things are going well and on schedule. Your focus should be particularly directed to your superiors at this point. If possible, seek audiences with management players who are key stakeholders of your work and who would need to know about your progress. Give lots of public praise to the people on your staff or the appropriate co-workers who have supported your work. Suggest to these supporters that they report how they have supported you. Remind them to include that they supported you in their monthly reports as this shows interdepartmental cooperation, a highly valued organizational characteristic in successful organizations.

As you declare your knowledge, the objective is simply to confirm beyond any doubt that putting you in this position was a smart decision. Once again, be direct and clear about your success by abandoning concerns about being called arrogant or manipulative by others. Authors Kathleen Ryan and Daniel Oestrich in their book, *Driving Fear Out of the Workplace*, say that "70% of people are afraid to speak up for fear of making career limiting utterances."

As a pioneer who is concerned about being viewed as arrogant, or who simply wants to calm your internal fears, you should look closely at the people you hold in high esteem or view as brilliant in their jobs or fields. Consider how these individuals gained your impression of their competence. Select and emulate the aspects of their behavior that you desire to possess. Inevitably, you will see that somehow they told you and others how competent they were. No doubt they communicated their competence to you in some confident, clear way. They may have demonstrated their competence to someone else and it was then relayed to you. What is the point that I'm making? You must be able to speak comfortably and confidently about yourself and to speak in glowing ways that express fully your knowledge, skills, and abilities. Robert Frost has said it best: "Something we were withholding made us weak, until we found out it was ourselves." Keep this thought in your mind and go forward!

Step 11

Ask for What You Want

After a year or more of proving yourself as a "first" to others and maybe even to yourself (I say this just to acknowledge that there still may be some doubt that creeps in occasionally), you will be so much wiser. With seasoning in your position, you will have a far greater understanding of the organization, the culture, how to get things done, the stated rules, the unwritten rules, and numerous other factors that occur. You still must perform strongly, of course, but at this point you will be seen primarily for your competence and not your "firstness." At this point, also, you should consider what you want from your current position and what your future might hold. Yes, you should be identifying your future needs, because your future positions should align with and support your personal vision. As you make this assessment be sure to look for connections to the organization's needs and how what you want for yourself might contribute to those needs. Recognizing this connection will help you articulate what you want next from the company. For instance, you might want to attend a financial executive program at Harvard University, take a sabbatical from your position, be placed on the new technology, or be sent to the annual sales convention. You may want tuition assistance to pursue an MBA, a transfer to another division in another state, pursuit of a special certification, or any number of things available in progressive organizations. Incidentally, if you are not in a progressive organization, you probably should pursue the door and leave because the longer you remain, the more stuck you will become.

Only you can determine what you want based on your needs assessment. But consider that you have done well and will continue to do well. You should look to sustain your success and ask for items that will assure that your knowledge, skills, and abilities grow and that your success and happiness continue.

Step 12

Look Beyond the Immediate Future

Too often, American businesses have avoided long-term planning in favor of entirely focusing on the short or near-term future. Gasoline prices have been escalating for decades and environmentalists, conservationists, and others have been suggesting, if not pleading, that we become energy efficient and much less energy-dependent as well. Automobile manufacturers continued to build cars larger, heavier, without corresponding fuel efficiency, and in any design as long as they could sell them immediately. This section is particularly straightforward and the message is to the point and reasonably brief but it has been dangerously ignored by Americans—stop thinking only of today and of the immediate future!

Cadillac Escalades and Hummers are two large sports utility vehicles (SUVs) that have become status symbols and sometimes statement vehicles. The 2008 Escalade averaged 14 miles per gallon (combined city and high-way) and the Hummers average fuel efficiency was even worse. There are numerous large cars yielding poor gas mileage but the real problem, as I see it, is that we keep building gas guzzlers and also that we haven't progressed better in making fuel efficient vehicles in the United States. The automobile industry has responded to such criticism in the past by claiming that Americans want these vehicles and if they want them, as a business, the responsibility was to build and profit from making them.

I understand the infatuation with the large comfortable SUV. I love the elevated view of the road that the sports utility vehicle provides and the ease of transporting a Christmas tree, but I want more miles per gallon! The statement the vehicles make for me if they do not get over 20 miles of gas per gallon, is not one of class, sophistication, or status; rather it is one of thinking for today only and when tomorrow comes, figuring it out. Too late! Furthermore, these vehicles said—loud and clear — that the American automobile industry valued immediate profits over long-term profits and energy independence for the United States.

In 2008, gas prices spiked to over $4.00 a gallon in most of the United States, but now that the prices have declined and hover around $2.00 per gallon, I fear that our short-term thinking will lead us back to the large fuel-inefficient SUVs, Escalades, and Hummers. However, the lower gas prices in combination with the huge downturn in the economy has resulted in more people thinking and looking a little farther toward the long-term. Kudos to these folks! We are all in this battle together. I'm speaking of the battle to be less dependent on middle-Eastern oil and much more independent, using United States energy, talent, and resources.

It seems to me that eighth grade civics students can understand the importance of winning this battle for our survival. Yet the people we elected to the congress 20 years ago and the American auto industry along with the

individuals who run our businesses and financial institutions, could not get the engineers and MBAs to win
this battle for the American driver and home owner.
They were too anxious to grab their corporate profits and
individual bonuses to be concerned with the threats of
energy dependence on countries and individuals that
envied our world economic position and, in some cases
did not like Americans.

Don't think that this tendency for short-term thinking has
not been insidiously passed on to you. We have all
been conditioned by this kind of thinking from years
when our economy was in good shape. You as a pioneer, however, should give some serious thought to your
longer-term organizational goals as well as your longer-
term personal goals. Often the personal goals will help
bring the organizational goals into sight. For example,
if your long-term personal goal is to be at the vice-pres-
idential level in a Fortune 500 company, then you must
assess your standing in your present position and company. If that seems to be out of the question in your

current organization, obviously you should be planning to move while first assessing why it is that you are "out of the question" and what you should do differently to get yourself into position at your new organization. Learn to think long term and not just short term. Bring your significant other or spouse in on the thinking as well.

Here is a long-term (5-10 years from now) planning process that can just as easily be used for short-term (2-3 years from now) planning. I know, 5-10 years from now is not that far away, but it is much farther away than most think about and I don't think I can persuade many readers to go beyond this point, based upon American living habits and practices.

1. Set your vision – What is your personal and professional long-term vision (5-10 years out)? Use the forms here to commit the plan to paper. The vision should be a word picture of what you want to be doing in both your personal and professional life.

2. Identify success factors - What are the critical factors needed to accomplish your vision? For example, personally, does it require that you stop renting and buy a house or condominium? Professionally, does it mean that you need to complete the MBA program from which you withdrew 2 years ago? List all of the critical success factors on both the personal and professional long-term planning sheets that follow.

3. Assessment of the environment – Scan your personal environment—e.g., house, family, kids, employment status, and your professional environment, e.g., still waiting for the promotion, pass the bar exam, gain more credibility at work —and write your assessment down.

4. Identify the gaps – In considering the previous environmental assessment, what are the gaps between your current circumstances and your long-term vision, both personally and professionally? List these gaps on your form.

5. Set objectives – Set your goals for each personal or professional gap that you have listed. A personal objective might be to save enough money for your two young children to go to college in 7 and 10 years respectively. A professional objective might be to move from being a market analyst to a marketing director in 10 years.

6. Take action steps – List the specific actions that you will take to accomplish your personal or professional objectives. For example, a personal action step might be to share your desire to complete the MBA with your significant other. A professional action step might be to make an appointment to speak with the admissions office and request paperwork from the graduate school.

7. Monitor your progress – Monitor your progress toward carrying out each step and adjust your plans as needed in order to accomplish your objectives. The monitoring step is extremely important and very often a reason for failing to meet and accomplish personal and professional objectives. Set time periods when you will monitor your progress on short-term or long-term goals. I've gone to school for so many years that I seem to psychologically and physiologically need to be doing something forward-looking each September, so I always monitor my personal and professional plans at that time. The other time I monitor my plans would be Super Bowl weekend. My friends don't get it and I don't either but it has become a time for reflection for me. I pull out my plans and monitor my progress in September and late January or early February, whenever the Super Bowl Game is scheduled. You should choose the time periods for yourself that make sense but you should at least monitor your progress twice a year. The important point is that whatever time and method you use, it should work. As a pioneer, monitoring your plan is one thing over which you have total control, so make the monitoring work and your plans will also work. And good luck!

Sample Long-term Planning Form
(Personal)

Vision (dreams of your personal life 5-10 years from now)

_____

_____

_____

_____

_____

Success factors (list the critical success factors needed to accomplish your personal vision)

_____

_____

_____

_____

_____

Environmental assessment (consider house, spouse, kids, friends other family, health)

_____

_____

_____

_____

_____

Gaps (between now and the vision of 10 years from now)

_____

_____

_____

_____

_____

Objective setting (list 5-7 goals that will close gaps)

_____

_____

_____

_____

_____

Action steps (list steps necessary to accomplish each objective)

_____

_____

_____

_____

_____

Sample Long-term Planning Form
(Professional)

Vision (dreams of your professional life 5–10 years from now)

_____

_____

_____

_____

_____

Success factors (list the critical success factors needed to accomplish your personal vision)

_____

_____

_____

_____

_____

Environmental assessment (consider your organization and workplace, your department, career field, professional network, house, spouse, kids, other family)

_____

_____

_____

_____

_____

Gaps (between now and the vision of 10 years from now)

_____

_____

_____

_____

_____

Objective setting (list 5-7 goals that will close gaps)

_____

_____

_____

_____

_____

Action steps (list the steps necessary to accomplish each objective)

_____

_____

_____

_____

_____

Afterward

You may have already discovered that I am a fan of Mark Twain, whose real name, of course, was Samuel Clemens. Why am I a fan? First, he traveled with great freedom and spirit on the Mississippi River, something that I would love to do. More importantly, he was a man who outgrew his racist views toward blacks and other minority group members; even more remarkably, he shared his "conversion" with the world in his writings. Have you done anything as courageous and profound? Have you known anyone who has done anything as profound?

Samuel Clemens was not a college graduate, but he saw reason to pay for the college education of two capable black men, one of whom graduated from Yale Law School. That individual became a judge and an eventual mentor to Thurgood Marshall, who became the first black Supreme Court justice. Clemens did not do this for publicity; in fact, there is no mention of it in his writings. In 1985, a Yale scholar discovered proof of Clemens's payments and a letter to the dean explaining his reasons. Clemens wrote that it was partial payment of the reparation *"due from every white man to every black man"* for the perpetration of the crime of slavery. (*The Wit and Wisdom of Mark Twain*, 1989)

In conclusion, I hope you have enjoyed reading about the black quarterback syndrome and have gained something from the read. Perhaps the book will provide you with companionship as it might have for Marlin Briscoe, Jackie Robinson, or Pee Wee Reese had it been available when they faced their challenges.

Norman M. Davis

Order Form

The Black Quarterback Syndrome_____$15.00

Quantity _____

Shipping/Handling
(Via U.S. Priority Mail)_____$4.00 each

Total_____$

PURCHASER INFORMATION

Name   :_____

Address:_____

_____

City:_____ State:_____

Zip Code:_____

Please mail Check or Money Order to:
Norman M. Davis
P.O. Box 3644
Woodbridge, CT 06525

172